Nathan Bedford Forrest & the Ku Klux Klan
YANKEE MYTH, CONFEDERATE FACT

LOCHLAINN SEABROOK WRITES IN THE FOLLOWING GENRES

Adult	Matriarchy
Alternate History	Men
American Civil War	Metaphysics
American History	Military History
American Politics	Mysteries and Enigmas
American South	Mysticism
Ancient History	Natural Health
Anthropology	Natural History
Apocrypha	Onomastics
Aviation	Paleography
Biblical Exegesis	Paleontology
Biblical Hermeneutics	Paranormal
Biography	Patriarchy
Children	Philosophy
Christian Mysticism	Photography
Coffee Table	Pictorial
Comparative Mythology	Poetry
Comparative Religion	Politics
Cooking	Prehistory
Cryptozoology	Presidential History
Diet and Nutrition	Quiz
Education	Reference
Encyclopediology	Religion
Entertainment	Revolutionary Period
Ethnic Studies	Science
Etymology	Scripture
European History	Self-help
Evolutionary Biology	Social Sciences
Exposés	Spirituality
Family Histories	Spiritualism
Film	Sport Science
Genealogy	Technology
Ghost Stories	Thanatology
Gospels	Thealogy
Health and Fitness	Theology
Historical Fiction	UFOlogy
Historical Nonfiction	Vexillology
History	Victorian Period
Humanities	War
Humor	Western
Illustrations	Wildlife
Law of Attraction	Women
Lexicography	World History
Life After Death	Young Adult

Mr. Seabrook does not author books for fame and glory, but for the love of writing and sharing his knowledge.

Be curious, not judgmental.

Nathan Bedford Forrest
and the
Ku Klux Klan

YANKEE MYTH, CONFEDERATE FACT

Excerpted from the author's work *A Rebel Born: A Defense of Nathan Bedford Forrest*, with new material & illustrations

Illustrated by the author, Colonel

Lochlainn Seabrook

JEFFERSON DAVIS HISTORICAL GOLD MEDAL WINNER

**Diligently Researched for the
Elucidation of the Reader**

Sea Raven Press, Nashville, Tennessee, USA

2015

NATHAN BEDFORD FORREST & THE KU KLUX KLAN

Published by
Sea Raven Press, LLC, founded 1995
Nashville, Tennessee, USA
SeaRavenPress.com

Copyright © 2015, 2016 Lochlainn Seabrook
in accordance with U.S. and international copyright laws and regulations, as stated and protected under the Berne Union for the Protection of Literary and Artistic Property (Berne Convention), and the Universal Copyright Convention (the UCC). All rights reserved under the Pan-American and International Copyright Conventions.

1st SRP paperback edition, 1st printing: December 2015, ISBN: 978-1-943737-11-6
1st SRP hardcover edition, 1st printing: December 2016, ISBN: 978-1-943737-40-6

ISBN: 978-1-943737-11-6 (paperback)
Library of Congress Control Number: 2015959041

This work is the copyrighted intellectual property of Lochlainn Seabrook and has been registered with the Copyright Office at the Library of Congress in Washington, D.C., USA. No part of this work (including text, covers, drawings, photos, illustrations, maps, images, diagrams, etc.), in whole or in part, may be used, reproduced, stored in a retrieval system, or transmitted, in any form or by any means now known or hereafter invented, without written permission from the publisher. The sale, duplication, hire, lending, copying, digitalization, or reproduction of this material, in any manner or form whatsoever, is also prohibited, and is a violation of federal, civil, and digital copyright law, which provides severe civil and criminal penalties for any violations.

Nathan Bedford Forrest and the Ku Klux Klan: Yankee Myth, Confederate Fact, by Lochlainn Seabrook. Includes an index, endnotes, and bibliographical references.

Front and back cover design and art, book design, layout, and interior art by Lochlainn Seabrook.
All images, graphic design, graphic art, and illustrations copyright © Lochlainn Seabrook.
Cover image: "Forrest and One of His Former Servants," by Lochlainn Seabrook.
Cover image and design copyright © Lochlainn Seabrook.
Portions of this book have been adapted from the author's other works

The views on the American "Civil War" documented in this book are those of the publisher.

The paper used in this book is acid-free and lignin-free. It has been certified by the Sustainable Forestry Initiative and the Forest Stewardship Council and meets all ANSI standards for archival quality paper.

PRINTED & MANUFACTURED IN OCCUPIED TENNESSEE, FORMER CONFEDERATE STATES OF AMERICA

Dedication

To the courageous white and black men and women who supported the original non-racist Ku Klux Klan against the constitutional illegalities, violent outrages, insidious immoralities, and high crimes and misdemeanors committed by the Liberal North during Reconstruction, 1865-1877.

Epigraph

"Many great monuments have been erected to Forrest's memory, but his greatest monument is erected in the hearts of the people of the Southland, whom he loved so well and served so faithfully."

Mrs. S. E. F. Rose, 1914

Contents

Notes to the Reader - 9
Introduction, by Lochlainn Seabrook - 13

1 POSTWAR FORREST: A NEW BEGINNING - 17
2 BIRTH OF THE RECONSTRUCTION KKK - 25
3 NORTHERN LIBERAL ACTIONS THAT LAUNCHED THE KKK - 45
4 CHARGES AGAINST FORREST CONCERNING THE KKK - 101
5 A SUMMARY OF FORREST & THE KU KLUX KLAN - 109

Appendix A: First Freedmen's Bureau Act, March 3, 1865 - 119
Appendix B: Second Freedmen's Bureau Act, July 16, 1866 - 121
Appendix C: First Reconstruction Act, March 2, 1867 - 127
Appendix D: Second Reconstruction Act, March 23, 1867 - 131
Appendix E: Third Reconstruction Act, June 19, 1867 - 137
Appendix F: Fourth Reconstruction Act, March 11, 1868 - 141
Appendix G: Reconstruction Speech of Thaddeus Stevens, Sept. 7, 1865 - 143
Appendix H: The Story of the Ku Klux Klan, by Thomas Dixon Jr. - 159
Appendix I: Prayer Offered at Pulaski, TN, KKK Birthplace Memorial - 167
Notes - 169
Bibliography - 176
Index - 183
Meet the Author - 187
Learn More - 189

Notes To The Reader

THE TWO MAIN POLITICAL PARTIES IN 1860
☛ In any study of America's antebellum, bellum, and postbellum periods, it is vitally important to understand that in 1860 the two major political parties—the Democrats and the newly formed Republicans—were the opposite of what they are today. In other words, the Democrats of the mid 19th Century were Conservatives, akin to the Republican Party of today, while the Republicans of the mid 19th Century were Liberals, akin to the Democratic Party of today.

Thus the Confederacy's Democratic president, Jefferson Davis, was a Conservative (with libertarian leanings); the Union's Republican president, Abraham Lincoln, was a Liberal (with socialistic leanings).[1] This is why, in the mid 1800s, the conservative wing of the Democratic Party was known as "the States' Rights Party."[2]

The author's cousin, Confederate Vice President and Democrat Alexander H. Stephens: a Southern Conservative.

Hence, the Democrats of the Civil War period referred to themselves as "conservatives," "confederates," "anti-centralists," or "constitutionalists" (the latter because they favored strict adherence to the original Constitution—which tacitly guaranteed states' rights—as created by the Founding Fathers), while the Republicans called themselves "liberals," "nationalists," "centralists," or "consolidationists" (the latter three because they wanted to nationalize the central government and consolidate political power in Washington, D.C.).[3]

Since this idea is new to most of my readers, let us further demystify it by viewing it from the perspective of the American Revolutionary War. If Davis and his conservative Southern constituents (the Democrats of 1861) had been alive in 1775, they would have sided with George Washington and the American colonists, who sought to secede from the tyrannical government of Great Britain; if Lincoln and his Liberal Northern constituents (the Republicans of 1861) had been alive at that time, they would have sided with King George III and the English monarchy, who sought to maintain the American colonies as possessions of the British Empire. It is due to this very comparison that Southerners often refer to the "Civil War" as the Second American Revolutionary War.

THE TERM "CIVIL WAR"
☛ As I heartily dislike the phrase "Civil War," its use throughout this book (as well as in my other works) is worthy of an explanation.

Today America's entire literary system refers to the conflict of 1861 using the Northern term the "Civil War," whether we in the South like it or not. Thus, as all book searches by readers, libraries, and retail outlets are now performed online, and as all bookstores categorize works from this period under the heading "Civil War," book publishers and authors who deal with this particular topic have little choice but to use this term themselves. If I were to refuse to use it, as some of my Southern colleagues have suggested, few people would ever find or read my books.

Add to this the fact that scarcely any non-Southerners have ever heard of the names we in the South use for the conflict, such as the "War for Southern Independence"—or my personal preference, "Lincoln's War." It only makes sense then to use the term "Civil War" in most commercial situations, distasteful though it is.

We should also bear in mind that while today educated persons, particularly educated Southerners, all share an abhorrence for the phrase "Civil War," it was not always so. Confederates who lived through and even fought in the conflict regularly used the term throughout the 1860s, and even long after. Among them were Confederate generals such as Nathan Bedford Forrest,[4] Richard Taylor,[5] and Joseph E. Johnston,[6] not to mention the Confederacy's vice president, Alexander H. Stephens.[7] Even the Confederacy's highest leader, President Jefferson Davis, used the term "Civil War,"[8] and in one case at least, as late as 1881—the year he wrote his brilliant exposition, *The Rise and Fall of the Confederate Government*.[9]

In 1895 Confederate General James Longstreet wrote about his military experiences in a work subtitled, *Memoirs of the Civil War in America*. Even the Confederacy's highest leader, President Jefferson Davis, used the term "Civil War,"[10] and in one case at least, as late as 1881—the year he wrote his brilliant exposition, *The Rise and Fall of the Confederate Government*.[11]

A WORD ON VICTORIAN MATERIAL
☛ In order to preserve the authentic historicity of the Civil War period, I have retained the original spellings, formatting, and punctuation of the

19th-Century individuals I quote. These include such items as British-English spellings, long-running paragraphs, and other literary devices peculiar to the time. Bracketed words within quotes are my additions and clarifications, while italicized words within quotes are (where indicated) my emphasis.

A WORD ON RACIST QUOTATIONS IN THIS WORK
☛ As part of my study on Forrest and the KKK I cite the words of several Caucasian 19th-Century men and women who evinced the typical white racial attitudes of their day, an attitude most obvious in Northerners like Abraham Lincoln: it was Dishonest Abe who, for example, not only regularly referred to American blacks as an "inferior race," barred them from the White House, repeatedly blocked black civil rights, and spent his entire adult life trying to deport them,[12] but it was he who, on July 17, 1858, said: "What I would most desire would be the separation of the white and black races."[13] This type of white bigotry was common and widespread in early America, particularly in the Northern states.

While the writing of this book necessitated that I quote such individuals in order to understand the sociopolitical soil in which the Reconstruction KKK germinated, it does not follow that I embrace such views. Anyone who is familiar with my literary work knows that I do not subscribe to any form of racism, and that, in fact, I eschew all aspects of racial bigotry (in whatever race they manifest) as unspiritual, ungodly, and un-Christian. Most importantly, racism is intellectually irrational and scientifically untenable, as my next entry shows.

A WORD ON RACE
☛ This work deals with Forrest and the KKK, both which the uninformed believe are "controversial subjects connected to white racism." Those who read this book from cover to cover, however, will quickly become disabused of these gross misconceptions. So as not to be tarred by the same broad brush, my views on the concept of race are germane here.

Contrary to popular opinion, and in particular the opinion of racists, there is no "race gene" that makes one white, black, red, yellow, or brown. There is no abrupt genetic line of demarcation between a Caucasian, a Negro, or an Asian. What actually exists is an infinite spectrum of human skin colors, from very white on one end to very black on the other, with every known color variation in between.

The reason for this is that we are all merely products of our ancestors and where and how they lived: generally speaking, the closer they dwelt to the heat and bright Sun at the equator the darker their skin and eyes, the curlier their hair, the taller their height; the further away they lived from the equator, the lighter their skin and eyes, the straighter their hair, the shorter their height.[14]

What we refer to as a "race" (an anthropologically obsolete word that has now been replaced by the more scientific term "ethnogroup") then is simply the end result of the human body's biological adaptation to environment; it is, in essence, a survival mechanism that has evolved over millions of years that has helped maintain and protect our species. To make anything else out of it is absurd, for the defining factor of our species is culture not biology.

In short, the very concepts of "race" and "racism" are delusions; nothing more than convenient but highly subjective, misleading, loaded, useless, and wholly unscientific methods of categorizing human beings by skin color.[15] Thus I reject the ambiguous concept of "race"; not on liberal moral principles, but on conservative scientific ones.[16] My use of the words race, racist, and racism throughout this book therefore is a concession to currently accepted social tradition and opinion, and does not reflect my personal view that there is only one true race: the human race.[17]

TO LEARN MORE

☞ Lincoln's War on the American people and the Constitution can never be fully understood without a thorough knowledge of the South's perspective. As this book's focus (Forrest and the original Ku Klux Klan) is quite narrow, and thus only provides a brief introductory guide to these topics, one cannot hope to learn the whole truth about them here. For those who are interested in a more in-depth study, please see my comprehensive histories, listed on page 2.

For a full treatment of Forrest's fascinating life story see my biography, *A Rebel Born: A Defense of Nathan Bedford Forrest*, from which some of *Nathan Bedford Forrest and the Ku Klux Klan* has been extracted.

Introduction

SOUTHERN HERO CONFEDERATE GENERAL NATHAN Bedford Forrest is disliked by the anti-South movement for a variety of reasons, most notably because he was white, Southern, and a slave owner and slave dealer. It is a fact, however, that he was a slave dealer for only seven years, and that he emancipated his slaves long before both the Civil War and Abraham Lincoln's fake and illegal Emancipation Proclamation.

We must add to this that at the time slavery was still legal under the Constitution across the entire United States—North and South, East and West—and that there were tens of thousands of black slave owners in America as well.

But since most pro-North advocates (and Liberals in general) detest facts almost as much as they detest the traditional South, these items of authentic history are routinely twisted, ignored, or suppressed, efforts to prevent them from getting out into the public forum.

Confederate General Nathan Bedford Forrest during Lincoln's War, circa 1864.

Aside from the Liberals' dissemination of both misinformation and disinformation regarding the General, arguably the number one reason the anti-Forrest movement is growing was his involvement with the Ku Klux Klan.

As we will explore in greater detail, the idea that Forrest started the KKK is pure Yankee mythology. The names of the six founders were long ago recorded and are well-known,[18] Forrest himself was not even aware of the group until at least one year after it was formed,[19] and he did not begin to openly support it until two years after was formed.[20]

Additionally, he could not have become involved with the KKK for racist reasons, as his critics charge, for it was not a racist organization.[21] Actually, it began as a type of self-protective police and social aid society, made up of both thousands of white *and* thousands of black members[22] (we even have evidence of an all-black Ku Klux Klan that operated out of Nashville), its original purpose being to help war widows and their children and to maintain law and order across the South[23] during the rise of Reconstruction tensions and escalating crime (remnants of Lincoln's illegal invasion, which had damaged much of the South's infrastructure).[24]

Indeed, in the genuine original KKK, or what I call the "Reconstruction KKK"—which lasted only a little over three years (late 1865-early 1869) and which is completely unconnected to today's KKK (which began in 1915)[25]—the main focus was on unscrupulous Northerners (known as "carpetbaggers") and on nefarious anti-South Southerners (known as "scallywags" or "home-Yankees") whatever their skin color, not on blacks specifically.[26]

It was only later, when carpetbaggers and scallywags encouraged the formation of the black Loyal Leagues—which were used to inculcate freed slaves in pro-North, anti-South propaganda and train them to use weapons and military tactics to taunt, punish, and even murder their former owners—that white KKK members began to understandably turn their attention toward African-Americans.[27]

Again, this was only for self-protection, not for racist purposes. Proof of this is that when carpetbag rule ended (about 1869), the original KKK immediately came to an end as well all across the "Invisible Empire" (i.e., the Southern states). In essence, when Southerners were allowed to take back political control of their own states there was no longer any need for an organization like the KKK.[28] As one historian put it: "When tranquility was restored to the land, the Klan 'folded their tents like the Arabs, and as silently stole away.'"[29]

Today's South-haters also delight in emphasizing "Forrest's role as Grand Wizard of the Klan." Sadly, this fiction has become so thoroughly entrenched that it was even believed by some Confederate soldiers well into the early 1900s.[30]

But in fact there is no irrefutable or even documentary evidence of this, as every Klansman took an oath of secrecy,[31] and none ever publically named their leader in print during the group's existence.[32] Indeed part of the Reconstruction KKK's original Constitution directed:

> That the origin, mysteries, and ritual, of this order shall never be written, but shall be communicated orally.[33]

It was George Washington Gordon (the man who some say introduced Forrest to the KKK)[34] who was grand wizard during the 1860s, not Forrest. Gordon's own wife, Ora Susan Paine, later testified to this fact.[35]

Some speculate that at most Forrest may have been the founder and Grand Dragon (leader) of the Tennessee chapter of the KKK.[36] But again, since nothing was ever written down there is no proof even of this theory,[37] and indeed, there is evidence that a man named Minor Meriwether started the Tennessee den.[38]

In his excellent 655-page Forrest biography, *Life of General Nathan Bedford Forrest* (1899) author John Allan Wyeth—who believed the General was too shrewd to associate himself with an "illegal" organization like the KKK[39]—devotes a mere single paragraph to Forrest's involvement with the group, with no mention of his being Grand Wizard.[40]

Likewise, Captain John W. Morton (another candidate for the man who introduced Forrest to the organization),[41] a noted Klan member and one who knew more about Forrest and this secret society than anyone else,[42] also wrote a book on the General without mentioning the KKK.[43]

In 1905, Thomas Dixon Jr. penned a novel called *The Clansman* (the basis for the 1915 film *Birth of a Nation*).[44] A fictionalized account of the development and life of the KKK, neither Forrest's name or even a hint of his personality, appear anywhere in the book.[45]

In 1871 and 1872, under oath, Forrest himself swore that he had not taken an active role in the organization,[46] and in fact had never even been a member, and only knew of it "from information from others."[47]

Whatever the actual facts it is safe to say that he played an important role of some type (most likely as simply a recruiter-advisor and a charismatic symbolic figurehead), for in March 1869, when various splinter groups began to grow racist and violent, a disappointed Forrest, the Klan's most well-respected, best known, and most influential associate, issued a "proclamation of dissolution," ordering the entire KKK to disband.[48]

From that moment on he forever disassociated himself from the organization.⁴⁹ A slanted South-loathing U.S. governmental committee later questioned Forrest, but found him innocent of any wrongdoing in connection with the Klan.⁵⁰ And there the matter stands, and ends.

South-haters, however, will not let go of the Forrest-as-racist-and-Grand-Wizard-of-the-KKK myth, and indeed they continue to perpetuate it, annually refueling it with new lies, new embellishments, and new fictions, all intended to permanently sully Forrest's reputation, racially divide America, and further humiliate the South.

In this small book I will debunk this anti-South fairy tale once and for all by examining both Forrest and the Ku Klux Klan without the baseless slander, distortions, sophistry, and dishonesty that normally accompany this topic. I will do this by using objective history and eyewitness testimony as a guide rather than emotion, opinion, political correctness, liberal ideologies, wishful thinking, dogmatic prejudice, presentism, and bias, as the anti-South movement traditionally does. In the process, the standard South-hating views of both Forrest and the original KKK will be utterly demolished, for, as will become clear, both are built on a tissue of lies.

To give context to this subject, and because the Reconstruction KKK was created due to the dire conditions that followed Lincoln's War, not only do I provide a substantial amount of material on the Reconstruction period, I begin this book with the General's life story beginning in the Spring of 1865, shortly after he surrendered to Union forces at Gainesville, Alabama, on May 9.

Refusing to believe or accept that Lee had surrendered a month earlier (on April 9), Forrest remained in the field hunting Yanks. It took a month, the inducement of his officers, and numerous threatening letters from U.S. officials before the natural born Rebel could be persuaded to hang up his famous Colt Navy Six Revolvers and accept that the War was indeed over—just one of the many reasons we Southerners will always idolize "Ol' Bedford."

Lochlainn Seabrook
Nashville, Tennessee, USA
December 2015

1

Postwar Forrest: A New Beginning

INTRODUCTION

THE DATE WAS JUNE 1865. Forrest's dazzling military career was now finished and he reentered the civilian world. His life, however, was about to become more colorful and controversial than ever before.

Tragically, as occurred with so many other Southerners, the War bankrupted the multimillionaire. And so now middle aged, war weary, suffering from serious wounds, and with little capital, Forrest faced the daunting and nearly incomprehensible task of starting his life over. Thanks to Lincoln, for the next ten years the General would live largely from "hand to mouth."[51]

Pasture lands at "Green Grove," Forrest's postwar plantation in Mississippi.

Fortunately for his family and the South, the word "impossible" was not in his vocabulary.[52] About this time a conciliatory Forrest remarked: "At one time I tried as hard as I could to help the South secede from the U.S. Now that the War is over," he continued, "I can say that it was a futile venture, and that I am now ready to stand up for the U.S.

government as enthusiastically as I once struggled against it."[53]

Yankee General William T. Sherman arrogantly predicted that the destitute Rebel would be forced to resort to a life of crime after the War.[54] Not only was this the last thing a man like Forrest would do, but the former Confederate chieftain actually had much working in his favor, despite his great financial losses.

Among his best assets were his personality, character, and reputation: Forrest had emerged from the War as the most important and popular man in Western Tennessee.[55] Even his former sworn enemies confirmed this. One of them, Union General Edward Hatch (a relative of today's Republican Senator Orrin Hatch of Utah), would later testify before the U.S. Congress that:

> There is no more popular man in West Tennessee to-day than the late rebel General Forrest. The quartermaster of my old regiment is partner with Forrest on a plantation; he said he took the plantation because Forrest is popular, and will take care of him and his interests.[56]

STARTING OVER

In late May 1865 Forrest left Grenada, Mississippi, with twenty of his former black servants and headed for Sunflower Landing, the site of his beloved 3,000-acre plantation, Green Grove. There, he and his wife Mary Ann set about repairing their lives, so rudely shattered by Lincoln's illicit war. First on the list was cleaning up the mess that resulted from his four-year absence.[57]

In September 1865, in an effort to bring in immediate cash, he repaired his steam saw mill and began selling a wide variety of lumber.[58] The rest of that autumn found Forrest harvesting corn while Mary Ann made butter and raised chickens.[59] Forrest described this period this way: "Immediately after the war, in 1866, I planted."[60]

Around this time he took up farming operations with a new business partner, a former Yankee officer named Major B. E. Diffinbach, from Missouri.[61] He also rented plantations and land to seven other former Union commanders,[62] who, a hospitable Forrest said, "made my house their home on Sundays."[63]

The General was obviously not one to hold a grudge, especially if there was money to be made.[64] And indeed money *was* made: by the end of 1867 he and Diffinbach had managed to turn a sizeable profit, and the General was financially solvent once again.⁶⁵ As before the War, he was helped in attaining this success mainly by blacks, not whites.

BLACK LABOR AT GREEN GROVE

When he reopened Green Grove many of Forrest's former black servants ("slaves" to Northerners) returned,⁶⁶ as did many of those that he had set free before Lincoln's War,⁶⁷ each one keen to become an employee of the man they had once called "Marse Bedford."⁶⁸

Southern blacks who remained faithful to Dixie and her people throughout and after the War were given the honorific title "Old Confeds,"⁶⁹ which ever after they wore proudly like an officer's medal. Those Old Confeds who returned to Forrest's farms all became loyal and productive postwar workers, bold facts that once again demolish the Yankee myth that he was a "sadistic racist." The story of Thomas ("Tom") Edwards, one of Forrest's black employees, is illustrative.

African-Americans played a large and positive role in Forrest's life, as he did in theirs.

When the General tried to prevent Edwards from beating his wife, the man turned on him with an axe. An unarmed Forrest wrenched the weapon from his attacker and buried it in his skull, killing him instantly. The next day a black judge examined the case and found that the General had acted in self-defense, all charges were dropped, and he was applauded by his other black employees for having rid the plantation of a mean, cruel, violent, temperamental, and dangerous individual.⁷⁰

Another indication of the way Forrest was seen by blacks—in

complete opposition to the anti-Forrest propaganda of Yankee mythology—was that around this time he offered to let his 200 black employees (all former slaves) out of their work contracts. Only eighteen (or 9 percent) opted to leave. The other 182 (91 percent) chose to stay on.[71]

Inquisitorial Yankee agents took notice. One, Union General Oliver O. Howard, commissioner of the notorious Freedmen's Bureau, met with Forrest. After examining his plantation's working conditions Howard noted that the former Rebel officer was doing all that he could to be just and equitable in the handling of his African-American employees.[72] Another, Captain Collis of Connecticut, visited Green Grove, after which he happily reported that General Forrest's management of his farm and black workers was the best he had ever seen, particularly concerning work hours, free time, and overall quality of life.[73]

Yet curiously, Collis, representing the U.S. government—the same body that had attacked Forrest for "racism" during the War—was also harshly critical of the General for his leniency toward his freed black workers. For one thing, the Yankee government did not approve of Forrest's habit of allowing them to carry guns and knives, both during work and at home.[74]

Northern military men also expressed grim dissatisfaction when they learned that he was making generous financial advances to his black employees. It was for granting these "injurious indulgences" that the U.S. government eventually ordered Forrest to cease and desist, with the veiled threat of severe repercussions if ignored.[75] Despite this overt racism from the North, and Forrest's obvious utter lack of prejudice, it is the latter who is routinely pilloried for being a "racial bigot." This is an example of what we here in the South call "Liberal hypocrisy."

FORREST IS "PARDONED" BY THE U.S. GOVERNMENT

In November 1866 Forrest wrote President Andrew Johnson, asking for "amnesty" for his "treason" against the United States. As Forrest, like all other traditional Southerners, never accepted Lincoln's ridiculous lie that the Confederacy was illegal (actually, it was Lincoln's invasion of the South that was illegal), this was no doubt one of the most difficult tasks the proud Southerner ever undertook.

The humiliation was doubled by the fact that it was not until July 1868, nearly two years later, that the "pardon" was issued. And while amnesty still granted him no political power (harsh Reconstruction laws prohibited Confederate officers from carrying firearms,[76] and from voting until 1870),[77] for many Northerners the reprieve helped repair some of the damage done to his image.

As such, in the eyes of some Yankees Forrest had by now become the model U.S. citizen and the very personification of a peace-loving reconstructed Rebel. As the General himself said:

> When the war closed I looked upon it as an act of Providence, and felt that we ought to submit to it quietly; and I have never done or said anything that was contrary to the laws that have been enacted.[78]

After the War Union General Frank P. Blair called Forrest "upstanding" and said that he regarded him "more highly than any man I have ever met."

Former Union General Frank P. Blair would have concurred. "Forrest," Blair said, "was the most influential man in all of West Tennessee, one who used his power only for peaceful purposes, spreading friendliness wherever he went. Not only was Forrest among the best soldiers in the Confederacy, but his upstanding attitude and compliant spirit since the end of the War has caused me to regard him more highly than any man I have ever met," the Yankee went on to comment.[79]

Forrest was indeed a changed man. In September 1869, at a barbeque near Gadsden, Alabama, he welcomed a group of Yankees from Massachusetts and Connecticut to the South, saying "this is the most honorable moment of my life, for it is a day when I can offer true comradeship to my Yankee brethren from the North. A momentous change has occurred: We are now one people, South and North," Forrest went on, "and it is time to meet the new challenge of reuniting the country."[80]

BACK TO MEMPHIS

In 1867, after two years at Green Grove, Forrest sold the plantation and returned to Memphis,[81] where he built a home on the Mississippi River and settled into the more predictable life of husband and townsman. Desperate to increase his income, he became president of a local fire insurance firm.[82] But the position does not seem to have lasted very long, for soon he began working on an idea he had had for some time: constructing a railroad line from Memphis to Selma, Alabama, in an effort to help rebuild the battered South.[83] Of this period in his life Forrest remarked:

Confederate Colonel Edmund W. Rucker, who lost his left arm due to an injury at the Battle of Nashville in December 1864, worked with Forrest after Lincoln's War.

> I want our country quiet once more, and I want to see our people united and working together harmoniously.[84]

Forrest's efforts resulted in the organization of the "Selma, Marion, and Memphis Railroad," of which he became president. One of his associates at the rail company was former Confederate Colonel Edmund Winchester Rucker,[85] like Forrest, a cousin of mine.[86]

The new rail endeavor would now enable him to earn a steady living. But it was more than just a business to Forrest. He also wanted to both help Dixie regain her prosperity and mend the enormous wound purposely created by Lincoln between South and North. As he later stated in 1872:

> I said when I started out with my roads that railroads had no politics; that I wanted the assistance of everybody; that railroads were for the general good of the whole country.[87]

As part of Forrest's plan to aid in the rebuilding of the nation, he hired some 400 blacks to work on his rail lines; not just as laborers, but also as architects, engineers, conductors, and foremen, jobs not available to blacks in the racist North at the time. Though the General was still considered a "bigot" by many bigoted Yanks, Southerners knew better: after his black employees' one-year contract ran out, all but fifteen returned to continue working for him.[88]

In other words, while only about 3 percent decided to leave, nearly 97 percent chose to remain with Forrest. This speaks volumes about how the General was actually viewed by African-Americans, yet this fact is completely disregarded by pro-North historians and the Liberal mainstream media.

During the postwar era blacks by the hundreds enthusiastically flocked to Forrest's plantations to work for the man they once knew as "Marse Bedford," belying the old Yankee myth of "Forrest the cruel racist and brutal slaver."

Enemies of the South have long wrongly confused the KKK that formed in 1865, what I refer to as the "Reconstruction KKK," with the modern or "New KKK" that formed in 1915—better known today as the "Knights of the Ku Klux Klan." Uninformed Liberals even mistakenly associate the Confederate Battle Flag with the New KKK, and of course white racism. Actually, the two organizations have almost nothing in common (except the name and regalia), the Reconstruction KKK was not an anti-black group (it was an anti-carpetbag one), and the primary flag used by the New KKK is the U.S. Flag (not the Confederate Flag)—as this photo of a 1925 Ku Klux Klan rally in Washington, D.C. clearly shows. Not even the Reconstruction KKK used the Confederate Battle Flag. Its official 1867 banner was the "Grand Ensign," a 3 foot by 5 foot triangular pennant with a black flying dragon in the center. This little book will aid in the education of the ignorant, the unlettered, and the unenlightened regarding Forrest and the two individual and unconnected Ku Klux Klans.

2

Birth of the Reconstruction KKK

FORREST, RECONSTRUCTION, & THE KKK

IT IS COMMONLY ASSERTED THAT around this time, in late 1865 or early 1866, Forrest founded the Pulaski Circle or Pulaski Den, or what would soon be given the odd name, the "Ku Klux Klan."[89]

The idea that Forrest started the KKK is an absurd fallacy that has been in existence for so long that it is now accepted as fact, not only by many of his modern relatives, but also by countless reputable Civil War authors and scholars. One can even still hear this old chestnut repeated by ignorant tour guides at historic sites across the South. To make matters worse, the Internet-savvy, anti-Forrest crowd has picked up on this falsehood, posting it online where it is now read by people around the globe as a genuine product of "scholarly research."

In actuality, as we will now prove, the organization was initiated by others, while Forrest only became associated with it much later.[90]

TRANSFORMATION OF THE ORIGINAL KKK

Though it was at first formed as a secret social society for the amusement and recreation of its largely playful, college-age members, when the North began passing a series of vicious and revengeful, anti-South Acts in March 1865 (see Appendices A, B, C, D, E, and F), the KKK began to transform into a political paramilitary body that sought to maintain law and order throughout the Confederate states during the postwar chaos.[91]

The original Reconstruction KKK was founded as a form of entertainment after the War ended. But this quickly changed when the Liberal North began to discuss passing a series of repressive, brutal, and unconstitutional "reconstruction" acts in the Conservative South. It was at this time that the Reconstruction KKK transformed into a Dixie-wide social aid and protective society, employing fear as its primary weapon. The aim of this mounted Klansman out of Tennessee, for example, was neither racism or violence, but rather simple intimidation of anti-South partisans (whatever their skin color) using strange costumes, bizarre language, and odd behavior. This approach worked brilliantly, helping end Yankee rule in much of the South in just three short years. By 1877 Reconstruction was dead, one of the greatest failures in U.S. history.

Packs of scallywags (anti-South Southern opportunists) and carpetbaggers (anti-South Northern opportunists), along with gangs of freed former slaves, were by now roaming the countryside, bribing, intimidating, extorting, pillaging, and even raping, torturing and killing, members of now disarmed and disenfranchised Confederate families.[92] Thousands of homes were burned down and countless farms, businesses, and lives were lost.[93] In Chicot County, Arkansas, for example, as Forrest himself observed, "bloodthirsty and riotous blacks" forced whites from their homes, robbed them, then burned their houses down, among "other lawless acts."[94]

Amidst the smouldering rubble armed Union forces stalked the streets of what was left of Southern towns, enforcing violent military rule upon an already humiliated and subjugated people. It should be noted that Northern military rule was deemed necessary because Yankees widely believed that Lincoln's (unconstitutional) invasion had totally destroyed the South's infrastructure. The South, so the North maintained, would now need to be "reconstructed"—a Yankee euphemism for Northernization.

But such was not the case. The South's infrastructure had not been "completely demolished," as many roads, bridges, railways, telegraph lines, water supplies, courts, stores, farms, markets, and plantations were still functioning. Furthermore, as all Southerners agreed, Dixie should have been left alone to rebuild herself. For many decades, however, the meddlesome North had already proven that it was incapable of minding its own affairs. And so the work of "reconstruction" began in earnest, literally the same day Lee stacked arms at Appomattox.

Lincoln's "Reconstruction" should be more properly called "Deconstruction," for far from being rebuilt, during this period the injured South was further brutalized by the North through abject neglect and vicious exploitation. (As proof we offer the following: in 1860 the bulk of the top ten most affluent states were in the South. Since the end of Lincoln's War in 1865, however, not a single state in Dixie has managed to achieve the national per capita income average. The effects of Lincoln's War are indeed with us still.)[95]

Thus began twelve additional years of horror, degradation, and sorrow across Dixie, a period I call "America's Reconstruction Holocaust," or more accurately, "the Second American Civil War."

As part of "Reconstruction," all of the Southern governments were "swept clean," and the South's minority of carpetbaggers, scallywags, and freed slaves were allowed to take over local politics. The new carpetbag-scallywag regime gave the vote to (largely illiterate) freedmen—though only if they agreed to cast their vote for the Republican ticket (then the Liberal Party). Yet this same right was now denied former Rebel soldiers and their families, intentionally setting the stage for continuing civil, racial, and social unrest between blacks and their former owners.

Incredibly, as if being disfranchised of all their civil rights was not enough, noble, brave, honest, and law-abiding Confederate officers, such as Forrest, Longstreet, and Lee, were considered "prisoners on parole," subject to impromptu arrest and imprisonment on charges of "treason" to the U.S. government.[96]

The new Reconstruction Acts (issued March 2, 1867; March 23, 1867; June 19, 1867; and March 11, 1868) called for a military state to be imposed on Dixie, which the North arrogantly divided into five "military districts," each headed by a Yankee officer and armed militia. Within these five districts local governments were subordinated to the central government in Washington, D.C. (yet another clear violation of the Constitution), which operated under the orders of the occupying Northern officers.[97]

Though Lincoln was by now dead (shot through the back of the head by a *Northerner*), many of his preposterous and illegal ideas were implemented, one of which was the "forty acres and a mule" directive: the North would "take over" (that is, steal) the plantations of former Confederates, divide them into smaller farms, and hand them out freely to former slaves.

Liberal Lincoln's new federate democracy (originally intended to be, and to remain, a confederate republic by the Founding Fathers)[98] added to the abasement by treating white Southerners as vanquished foreigners in their own land, even unlawfully pushing through the Fourteenth Amendment of the Constitution at gunpoint, all against the will of the Southern people.[99] According to the Constitution, the U.S. government was supposed to be protecting its citizens. Instead, it was oppressing them.[100] Along with the inevitable political corruption and judicial anarchy brought on by the carpetbag-scallywag regime, the once rich Southland began sinking into unmitigated poverty.[101]

U.S. President Abraham Lincoln, who had long cruelly campaigned to have the South subdued, industrialized, and Northernized, perished before he could see his harsh Reconstruction plans go into effect. Unfortunately for Dixie, the Radical South-haters who succeeded him initiated even stricter, far more savage Reconstruction policies after his death, sparking the formation of the original Ku Klux Klan in late 1865.

Thus was laid the groundwork for the birth of the Reconstruction KKK, a Conservative Southern effort to combat the unconstitutional crimes being waged against Dixie by the Liberal North.

THE KKK: ITS NAME, METHODS, PURPOSE, & CONSTITUTION

The group took its name from the Greek word *kuklos*, meaning a "circle" (that is, a "circle" of protection), to which was added the word "klan," giving it an esoteric air of mystery, secrecy, fearsome power, and supernatural authority.[102] Members played up these characteristics in an attempt to strike fear into the hearts of their sworn enemies: carpet-baggers and scallywags, wherever their birthplace, whatever their skin color.

One method was the wearing of long white robes, masks, and conical hats (designed and sewn by Southern women, mainly the wives of former Confederate soldiers), and the prominent use of strange words and occultic writings—the latter often accompanied by grim illustrations of a skull and crossbones, hanged men, coffins, and the direful admonition: "BEWARE!"[103]

Silent midnight marches through town on horseback (with the horses themselves draped in long flowing white sheets) were calculated to display an irresistible otherworldly show of force. Sometimes scores of eerie masked riders would descend on "Pow Wows," outdoor meetings of white and black scallywags and carpet-baggers, in order to "put the fear of God" in them. Aided by loyal black Southern spies, just one of these visits from the white-robed "ghouls" would put an end to all future Pow Wows in the area and prompt enemies of the South to move somewhere else—the very purpose of the ruse.[104]

Though all of this was primarily bluff, it was successful in working overtime on the imaginations of the naive, the superstitious, and the illiterate. However, those who actually violated the South and her people in some serious way could be, and often were, met with immediate justice and frightful retribution. This was a war after all.[105]

These activities tie in perfectly with the Klan's sole function at the time: to act as a self-policing, relief-and-aid society for the protection and care of all Southern families, particularly those made homeless and jobless by Lincoln's War.[106] The Reconstruction KKK became, in other words, "the salvation of the South," for it was founded on the "sacred principles" of the "love and protection of home."[107] As one former KKK member put it:

> We were law-abiding citizens, and were organized only for the

protection of our women, children, and homes, and to enforce the law and insist on its enforcement.[108]

Forrest himself accurately called it a "protective, political, military organization,"[109] maintaining that it was

> intended as a defensive organization to offset the Union League; to protect ex-Confederates from extermination by [Liberal Tennessee Governor William G.] Brownlow's militia; [and] to prevent the burning of [Southern] gins, mills and residences.[110]

To get a better understanding of the Reconstruction KKK let us look at the group's Constitution, which laid out its "objects" in plain language:

> *This is an institution of Chivalry, Humanity, Mercy, and Patriotism:* embodying in its genius and principles all that is chivalric in conduct, noble in sentiment, generous in manhood, and patriotic in purpose; its peculiar objects being:
> First—To *protect the weak, the innocent, and the defenseless*, from the indignities, wrongs and outrages, of the lawless, the violent and the brutal, to *relieve the injured and oppressed*, to *succor the suffering and unfortunate*, especially the widows and orphans of Confederate soldiers.
> Second—To *protect and defend the Constitution of the United States*, and all laws passed in conformity thereto, and to protect the States and the people thereof from all invasion from any source whatever.
> Third—*To aid and assist in the execution of all constitutional laws*, and to protect the people from, unlawful seizure, and from trial except by their peers in conformity to the laws of the land.[111]

The Reconstruction Klan's Creed noted its relationship to God and to the U.S. government and Constitution:

> We, the Order of the Ku Klux Klan, reverentially acknowledge the majesty and supremacy of the Divine Being, and recognize the goodness and providence of the same. And we recognize our relation to the United States Government, the Supremacy of the Constitution, the Constitutional Laws thereof, and the

Union of States thereunder.[112]

That obedience to the U.S. Constitution was paramount can be seen in the order's oath, which included the following declaration, required of all prospective members:

> I promise and swear that I will uphold and defend the Constitution of the United States as it was handed down by our forefathers in its original purity.[113]

This KKK "warning" is typical of the type of missive a carpetbagger or scallywag could expect to find pinned to his front door in the middle of the night. Its weird but mostly meaningless images and strange words, meant to scare the recipient from the area if not the South, worked like magic on all but the most incorrigible ruffians—who would require more forceful "convincing." The text scribbled crudely under the above drawings reads: "When you are in Calera we warn you to hold your tongue and not speak so much with your mouth or otherwise you will be taken on surprise and led out by the Klan and learnt to stretch hemp. Beware. Beware. Beware. Beware. Bloody Bones."

At the formation of a Klan in South Carolina in January 1871, all in attendance agreed to the begin their den's credo with the following clause:

> The fundamental creed of this association is: first, *justice*; second, *humanity*; third, *constitutional liberty* as bequeathed to us by our forefathers.[114]

This sentiment was repeated in thousands of KKK circles across the

South between 1865 and 1869.

From these few examples alone it is clear that the original KKK, with which Forrest was associated, was nothing like the fabricated fantasy version that is still being promulgated by the anti-South movement: that it was a lawless, racist, anti-American band of white thugs, bigots, murderers, and felons. As with all *conservative* organizations then as now, the Reconstruction KKK was concerned both with law and with obedience to law, and more specifically constitutional law. This is quite in opposition to *liberal* organizations, which focus on nebulous concepts like "justice," "equality," and "fairness," all terms that are highly subjective and arbitrary—thus the need for objective fundamental laws, like the Constitution, that apply to all people in all circumstances.

THE KLAN'S REAL ENEMY

The true aim of the Reconstruction KKK is easily proven by examining who it was that it sought to "protect." Its security forces did not just look out for the welfare of whites. They also defended blacks as well. For contrary to Northern folklore the original KKK was not an anti-black organization. It was an anti-Yankee organization;[115] or more specifically, an anti-carpetbagger, anti-scallywag, anti-Northern Liberal (known at the time as "anti-Republican")[116] organization. After being constantly attacked with the accusation "you Southern people hate negroes!" one former white Southern member of the *modern* KKK responded this way:

> The best people of the South not only do not hate [the] . . . negro but *they hold him in high esteem.* The better class of Southern white man is the best friend the negro race has in this country today.[117]

This was just as true in the 1860s as it is today, for as Alexis de Tocqueville and many other famed early writers noted, the South has always been more racially tolerant than the North.[118] This explains why there were thousands of black members in the original Reconstruction KKK,[119] and also why Southern African-Americans often aided white KKK chapters[120] by spying on fellow blacks who had become scallywags, recording their whereabouts, meeting places, and activities.[121]

Not surprisingly there was an all-black KKK den that operated in the Nashville area,[122] one which worked in conjunction with all-white chapters to combat the nefarious effects of Reconstruction and what I call "carpetbaggism": a Liberal Northern movement, *still going strong today*, to destroy Southern pride, rewrite Southern history, suppress Southern heritage, marginalize the Southern people, and fully Northernize and industrialize Dixie.

This illustration, from 1868, reveals the true enemy of the Reconstruction KKK: it was not blacks, but *carpetbaggers* (hanging on right), treacherous Northern whites who came South after the War in order to prey on the ravaged region, and *scallywags* (hanging on left), turncoat Southerners brainwashed by Yankee myth and who sided with the Liberal North.

Victorian Southerners of all races, in particular Reconstruction KKK members, were not amused by this Yankee meddling and insolence, and banded together to fight their common enemy. Thus one Southern historian noted that:

> Many instances could be related of the good done by the [Reconstruction] Ku Klux, for, in every instance, *they protected the just rights of the negro as well as the whites*, and they stood always for the protection of the menaced life, liberty, and property, of *all* innocent men.[123]

As we will see shortly, "General Order Number One," issued by the Reconstruction KKK in Tennessee in 1869, provides ample evidence for this statement, declaring that the Klan was essentially, originally, and inherently a protective organization. It proposes to execute law instead of resisting it; and to *protect all good men, whether white or black, from the outrages and atrocities of bad men of both colors*, who have been for the past three years a terror to society and an injury to us all.[124]

The non-racist position of the original KKK was summed up by Forrest himself. In 1872, when asked who the order was supposed to protect its members from, he replied, "from anybody."[125]

THE RECONSTRUCTION KKK WINS FORREST'S PATRONAGE

Forrest, like so many of his neighbors, was quick to support the fledgling organization, which immediately set up "dens" in various Tennessee towns such as Franklin, Columbia, Shelbyville, and Nashville. With their homes, livelihoods, lives, and very culture at stake, his decision is not difficult to understand, especially from a 21st-Century perspective. Who today would not want to do all they could to protect the innocent, the injured, the sick, the weak, the elderly, the widowed, the orphaned, and the dispossessed under the same circumstances?

Both the KKK and Dixie, in turn, were glad to receive Forrest's support, for he was widely known for "his ability, his integrity, his unselfish devotion to the Southern people, and his desire to aid them in great crisis."[126] As even one anti-KKK historian noted, General Nathan Bedford Forrest was

> one of the most distinguished and capable officers in the late Confederate army, and [is] recognized today among military students as one of the foremost cavalry leaders of all times. . . . A careful search of every available record fails to reveal that he ever received one penny as compensation for his labors, or that his [efforts on behalf of the Klan] . . . ever brought him any gifts, perquisites, or emoluments. His military title was unimpeached, his last commission being that of lieutenant-general. He never called himself "Emperor," never signed any of his official orders as "His Majesty," and never assumed any of the titles or styles of royalty. He was a plain, unassuming soldier and gentleman, who, having a great task to perform, did his work gratuitously and from motives of patriotism only, and then, the work having been completed,

disbanded . . . [the] organization and retired. . . . *Forrest, as far as can be ascertained, served his country for patriotism.*[127]

Forrest, shown here after the War, understandably and fully supported the ambitions of the Reconstruction KKK, and gladly lent his name and influence to the conservative Southern organization.

In a speech at Brownsville, Tennessee, in the summer of 1868, addressing both whites and blacks, Forrest said that he supported any organization that would help guard his people, offer police protection, and maintain the South's constitutional rights: "Lincoln's War," he asserted, "took everything from us but our honor. It is now time to defend our spouses, our loved ones, and our region from further depredations."[128]

Forrest's sponsorship, fame, and reputation lent cachet to the Reconstruction Klan and in 1867, at the Nashville KKK Convention, some say that he was made the first Grand Dragon of the Tennessee chapter. But unfortunately for those making this claim, indisputable evidence for it does not exist.[129]

What is known is that his affiliation with the organization by this time had drawn thousands of new recruits until, at its zenith, the organization had an official membership of nearly 600,000 individuals nationwide,[130] including thousands of Northerners.[131] The South was rising up in pride and defense against an overwhelming occupying force whose publically stated goal was to destroy not only the very heart and soul of Dixie, but also its economic and political power.

RECONSTRUCTION TAKES A TURN FOR THE WORSE
Throughout the War Liberal Northern interests had been bribing and intimidating blacks to foment violence and insurrection against their

former masters, using the Loyal League (or Union League or Black Loyal League, as it was also called), to hide their anti-South activities.¹³² By 1869 the result was an explosion of race riots and racial tensions across the South, particularly in Georgia, where the mugging of white men and the raping of white women by blacks had become commonplace.¹³³

As anti-white hate crimes by racist blacks peaked, elements of the KKK grew increasingly hostile toward African-Americans (the William Lloyd Garrison-inspired Nat Turner Rebellion of 1831, in which roving gangs of black supremacists and black racists indiscriminately murdered white families, had not yet been forgotten thirty-eight years on). Out of fear and in retaliation, commensurate harassment and murder of blacks by some KKK members (as well as "imposters" claiming to be members) began in earnest.¹³⁴ Their crimes, however, soon became just as heinous as those committed by Northern reconstructionists against the South.¹³⁵

The author's cousin Confederate General George Washington Gordon is said to have introduced Forrest to the KKK in 1866 or 1867. According to credible testimony, Gordon, who once served as Commander-in-Chief of the United Confederate Veterans (the forerunner of today's Sons of Confederate Veterans) was the first and only Grand Wizard of the Reconstruction KKK, not Forrest. Gordon was later elected a Tennessee Congressman.

As he watched this violence grow, an indignant Forrest, the Klan's most influential supporter, tried to quell "outrages" by both whites *and* blacks.¹³⁶

FORREST CLOSES DOWN THE RECONSTRUCTION KKK

This effort having failed, in January 1869 he issued "General Order Number One," which commanded the entire organization to dissolve.¹³⁷ The KKK, Forrest declared, had become "perverted from its original honorable and patriotic purposes," becoming "injurious instead of subservient to the public peace and public safety for which it was intended."[138]

Additionally, he noted, it was no longer needed because the KKK had accomplished its main objectives: to overthrow the carpetbag-scallywag regime and restore civilization and power to the South.[139] Or as Forrest himself put it, the dissolution of the KKK was necessary because:

> There was no further use for it . . . the country was safe . . . there was no apprehension of any [more] trouble.[140]

When asked if the KKK had proven beneficial to the South in any way, Forrest replied:

> No doubt of it. Since its organization the [Loyal] leagues have quit killing and murdering our people. There were some foolish young men who put masks on their faces and rode over the country frightening negroes; but orders have been issued to stop that, and it has ceased.[141]

Contrary to Northern anti-South folklore, when Forrest ordered the Reconstruction KKK shut down, he meant just that: according to his own testimony, and probably his own personal order,

> three members of the Ku-Klux have been court-martialed and shot for violations of the orders not to disturb or molest people.[142]

This is not the Forrest of Northern myth. It is the Forrest of Southern reality. Here is the full text of "General Order Number One":

> Whereas, information of an authentic character has reached these head-quarters that the blacks in the counties of Marshall, Maury, Giles, and Lawrence are organized into military companies, with the avowed determination to make war upon and exterminate the Ku Klux Klan, said blacks are hereby solemnly warned and ordered to desist from further action in such organizations, if they exist.

The G. D. (Grand Dragon) regrets the necessity of such an order. But this Klan shall not be outraged and interfered with by lawless negroes and meaner white men, *who do not and never have understood our purpose.*

Contrary to popular opinion the Reconstruction KKK had no set uniform or outfit. Klansmen could design and wear whatever they liked, the weirder the better. These two costumes, from an 1867 den in Alabama, were made, as nearly all were, by Southern women.

In the first place *this Klan is not an institution of violence, lawlessness, and cruelty; it is not lawless; it is not aggressive; it is not military; it is not revolutionary.*

It is essentially, originally, and inherently a protective organization; it purposes to execute law instead of resisting it, and *to protect all good men, whether white or black, from the outrages and atrocities of bad men of both colors,* who have been for the past three years a terror to society, and an injury to us all.

The blacks seem to be impressed with the belief that this Klan is especially their enemy. We are not the enemy of the blacks, as long as they behave themselves, make no threats upon us, and do not attack or interfere with us.

But if they make war upon us, they must abide the awful retributions that will follow.

This Klan, while in its peaceful movements and disturbing no one, has been fired into three times. This will not be endured any longer; and if it occurs again, and the parties be discovered, a remorseless vengeance will be wreaked upon them.

We reiterate that we are for peace and law and order. No man, white or black, shall be molested for his political sentiments. This Klan is not a political party; it is not a military party; it is a protective organization, and will never use violence except in resisting violence.

Outrages have been perpetrated by irresponsible parties in the name of this Klan. Should such parties be apprehended, they will be dealt with in a manner to insure us future exemption from such imposition. *These impostors have, in some instances, whipped negroes. This is wrong! Wrong! It is denounced by this Klan as it must be by all good and humane men.*

The Klan now, as in the past, is prohibited from doing such things. We are striving to protect all good, peaceful, well-disposed, and law-abiding men, whether white or black.

The G. D. deems this order due to the public, due to the Klan, and due to those who are misguided and misinformed.

We therefore request that all newspapers who are friendly to law, and peace, and the public welfare, will publish the same. By order of the G. D., Realm No. 1.[143]

We will note here that Forrest does not name Tennessee's Grand Dragon (a state KKK leader) and speaks of this man in the third person. Obviously he was speaking *for* the leader, not *as* the leader himself.

Whatever the identity of the group's head, by the early Spring of 1869 the original Ku Klux Klan, "which gave its name to the secret movement which began the undoing of Reconstruction, ceased to exist as an organized body."[144]

THE POST KKK PERIOD

The consummation of the KKK's aims came when the much reviled, Radical Liberal, New South Tennessee Governor William G. Brownlow, resigned to become a U.S. senator. The horrors of "Brownlowism" were finally over.[145] The new governor, DeWitt C. Senter, took office in February 1869, after which he dropped the voting ban against former Confederates, who duly aided him in winning the state election in August 1869.[146]

Despotic scallywag William Gannaway Brownlow, arch nemesis of Forrest and the Reconstruction KKK. It was Tennessee Governor Brownlow who disenfranchised former Confederate supporters then gave the right to vote to illiterate blacks in the Volunteer State. He also banned the wearing of Confederate uniforms and instituted a "state guard" whose main purpose was to torment and provoke KKK members. Little wonder that Tennessean Forrest despised Brownlow, or that the Radical Liberal Unionist received constant death threats from Klansmen.

Forrest was now free to speak his mind publically without fear of arrest by Brownlow and his henchmen, who had been mercilessly arresting KKK members and harassing former Confederate soldiers and officers. To whites and blacks everywhere, the politically conservative General said: "Let's get rid of both the Ku Klux Klan *and* the Loyal League. Both have become unnecessary. Let us join together as one nation."[147]

Then as now, Conservatives sought to unite Americans; then as now Liberals sought to divide Americans.

Unfortunately Forrest was ignored, and the Klan continued on under various names (for example, the Constitutional Union Guards, the Pale Faces, the White Brotherhood, the White League, and the Knights of the White Camelia)[148] until around 1880, when "all these organizations gradually went out of existence."[149] In October 1915 the modern KKK was established by Colonel William Joseph Simmons of Atlanta, Georgia, flourishing into the present day under the name the "New KKK," or Knights of the Ku Klux Klan.[150]

THE DIFFERENCE BETWEEN THE ORIGINAL RECONSTRUCTION KKK & THE MODERN NEW KKK

Let us record here that the "Old KKK" of late 1865, that is, the Reconstruction KKK, is in no way linked to the "New KKK," that is, the modern KKK of today. The two could not be more "different in conception, organization and purpose."[151] Indeed, it is the height of irony that among Forrest's greatest critics are those who support full civil rights for all people. And yet this was one of the main purposes of the Reconstruction KKK, the organization which Forrest supported.

He detested the intolerance, racism, and violence that later crept into the KKK, which is why he eventually both disassociated himself from it and ordered it to break up and disperse. As such, the Reconstruction KKK, which lasted a mere three years and four months (December 1865-March 1869) and the modern KKK (post 1915-present) are in no way connected and should not be confused with one another, as is routinely done by enemies of the South. The former, after all, was only meant to be a *temporary* self-protective police and social aid society that served *all races* during the first three years of Reconstruction. The latter, however, was founded as a *"lasting"* fraternal order whose primary goal was to encourage American patriotism and the "preservation of pure Anglo-Saxon institutions, ideals, and principles." And though it is true that the modern KKK was meant to be

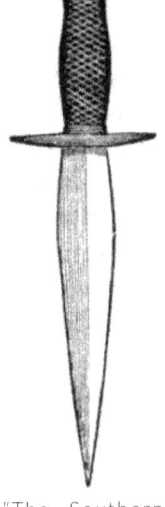

"The Southern Cross," one of the many symbols used by the Reconstruction KKK in its ceremonies.

> a living memorial to the old [Reconstruction] Klansmen . . . there was no thought in the mind of [its founder] Colonel Simmons to revive in any way the night-riding, masked operations of the original Ku Klux Klan, for conditions in the South do not justify such an organization today.[152]

Obviously, Forrest played no role whatsoever in the development of the modern KKK,[153] which arose nearly 40 years after his death. And we can be certain that he would not be a member of it if he were alive today. In fact, he would have repudiated such an organization, just as he did in 1869 when racial intolerance, and its accompanying violence, began to manifest in the Reconstruction KKK.

HOW IMPOSTERS HURT THE KLAN'S REPUTATION

Adding to the confusion over the true functions and purposes of the Reconstruction Klan was the fact that many individuals who were *not* members pretended to be in order to cover up their various crimes and divert blame onto the organization.

Individuals sometimes impersonated Reconstruction KKK members in order to hide their immoral deeds against minorities and others. This practice wreaked havoc within the real Klan—which thoroughly repudiated violence and racism—and tainted its image and reputation with the public. Even worse, it is the illegal and violent legacy left behind by these imposters which modern day Liberals have pinned on Forrest and the Reconstruction KKK. The facts are that the General severely denounced such acts and the Klan itself issued the death penalty for anyone violating its strict rules of conduct.

The deception worked. To this day South-hating Yanks and Liberals still associate and confuse the crimes of these disreputable imposters with the Reconstruction KKK, which was initiated and operated by law-abiding, conservative Southern "gentlemen of education and refined tastes."[154] Historian Mrs. S. E. F. Rose (neé Laura Martin) comments on this particular problem:

Many outrages were committed in the name of the Ku Klux, by parties who did not belong to the Klan; reckless firebrands, with private hatreds to appease, and having the audacity to call themselves Ku Klux. Thus the impression was made that the Ku Klux were a set of vicious men with no regard for law and order; but these outrages were committed by bands of thieving Scalawags, who used the name as a cloak for their evil deeds. *No genuine Ku Klux would have been guilty of a deed or an act that would bring the blush of shame to any brave or honorable man. They belonged to the best class of citizens, once soldiers of the Confederacy, who had only the best interests of society in view, and would scorn to do a mean or cowardly act. . . . It would be very unjust and unfair to place upon the real Ku Klux the odium of these evil deeds, which were deeply regretted by them, but impossible to control.*[155]

The anti-South movement has, of course, used the accounts of these nefarious impersonators to its advantage in its war on Dixie and her traditional family, religious, and political values. But this is to be expected from a group that cannot abide reality, shuns facts for fantasy, and thinks nothing of rewriting authentic history to suit its leftist views.

Pro-North advocates do not want you to know that Southern blacks, like this former female "slave," often aided the Reconstruction KKK.

A group of white and black Liberal South-haters at a political convention in 1875. Known as "Reconstructionists," such highly partisan groups worked tirelessly to overthrow the Southern political system and destroy white Southern culture. As with interfering intolerant Liberals today, the goal of the Leftist Reconstructionists was to rid the South of all traces of Southernness and Confederate imagery and force Northern ideas on Dixie; in other words, make the informal, leisurely, nonconformist, agricultural, religious South into an exact replica of the reserved, fast-paced, conformist, industrial, agnostic North. They began by rewriting American history, particularly Civil War history, in order to hide, suppress, and obliterate the truth about the conflict. In the process they turned the Confederacy into a "treasonous and illegal rebellion" and the Reconstruction KKK into a "murderous band of racist hooligans," absurd myths that continue to be widely disseminated by mainstream writers, historians, and publishers. Though there are untold thousands of ignorant and prejudiced individuals responsible for what I call "The Great Yankee Coverup" (see my book of the same name), just as a fish rots from the head down, one must look to the leader of the anti-South movement for the root cause, and that leader was Abraham Lincoln. It was Dishonest Abe who first officially demonized the Confederate Battle Flag when, on September 11, 1863, the infamous big government Liberal arrested and deported a group of Maryland publishers for printing a poem about our beautiful starry banner called "The Southern Cross." His subsequent anti-South activities and policies gave permission to other South-loathing progressives who came after him to meddle in Southern affairs, edit Southern history, and impose Yankee dogma on Dixie, a villainous practice more acceptable now that even at the time of Lincoln's War. Our sixteenth president's true motivations were unveiled in 1862 when he told Interior Department official T. J. Barnett that he planned to change the character of the War to one of "subjugation." "The South," Lincoln told his startled listener, "is to be destroyed and replaced with new propositions and ideas." The "Civil War" is indeed still being waged, not with guns and cannon, but now with words and ideas. It was and is, after all, merely a continuation of the world's oldest battle: Conservativism versus Liberalism.

3

Northern Liberal Actions That Launched the KKK

THE TRUTH ABOUT SO-CALLED "RECONSTRUCTION"

IN ORDER TO BETTER UNDERSTAND the reasons the original Ku Klux Klan was formed, as well as why the Southern people united behind it, let us now examine the Reconstruction period as described by actual Klan members, anti-KKK writers, Southerners, Northerners, men, women, and pre-1900 individuals and post-1900 individuals. One cannot hope to comprehend Forrest's support of the KKK without a thorough knowledge of what inspired its creation.

Reconstruction would be more properly called "Deconstruction." Fortunately for the South it failed, thanks in large part to the courageous efforts of Forrest and the Reconstruction KKK.

As will become patently clear, the 12-year period of Reconstruction (1865-1877) was little more than a continuation of the War itself (1861-1865), which had been initiated by the North to begin with, and which was prolonged afterward by the North as a vengeful form of retaliation on the Southern people for daring to break from the Union. This makes the "Civil War" not four years in duration, as our deceitful mainstream historians have long claimed, but 16 years long, from 1861 to 1877.

AMERICA'S SECOND CIVIL WAR

I would go one step further in describing Reconstruction as "America's Second Civil War" (which, revealingly, is similar to what some Yankees called it)[156] and the Reconstruction KKK "the Second Confederate Army." For, like the first illegal invasion of Dixie—which Lincoln and his cohorts devilishly disguised as a war to "preserve the Union" and "destroy slavery"—it was a Liberal Northern effort to *overturn* the Constitution and a Conservative Southern effort to *uphold* the Constitution, this time camouflaged as a Yankee "charity" known as "Reconstruction."

The Battle of Fort Sumter was instigated by Lincoln, who tricked the South into firing the first shot in order to "make it appear that the South was the aggressor," and thus responsible for the Civil War. Another Yankee lie.

Not satisfied to have beaten the South militarily, Reconstruction was the North's chance to now beat her politically, socially, and financially, an opportunity that was not to be missed if the Yankee's true goal was to be fully realized: the total obliteration of the South as a distinct region of the country, along with the complete Northernization of the South and her people.

THE WAR SET THE STAGE FOR RECONSTRUCTION

These facts will become increasingly obvious as one learns more about what actually went on behind so-called "Reconstruction"—arguably one of the worst debacles in American history; an era of ongoing Southern humiliation and brutal punishment that would be more correctly named "Deconstruction."

As you read the following statements and eyewitness accounts (in conjunction with the appendices) by those who survived both Lincoln's War and Reconstruction, try to imagine yourself living in the South in the mid to late 1860s. You have just endured four bloody years of an illegal invasion by hostile, aggressive, Liberal Yankee do-gooders, whose crimes against both Confederate soldiers and Southern civilians not only violated the Geneva Conventions, but every standard of morality, ethics, religion, and common decency.

Beginning on April 12, 1861 (at the Battle of Fort Sumter), for nearly 1,500 days you have watched as your family members, friends, and neighbors were illegally arrested and imprisoned, or worse, tortured, raped, and killed. For four years you have lived in intimate contact with the sounds of marching troops, rifles, cannon, and death, as well as the smell of gun smoke and dead bodies in the air. You have suffered the death of your father, husband, son, brother, or lover on the battlefield. You have stood by as your home was ransacked and burned to the ground by Union soldiers, your barn, granary, and stables pillaged, your livestock stolen, your pets and even black servants shot down in cold blood.

Carey Street, Richmond, Virginia, April 1865, shortly after Lee's surrender. Pro-North historians and Liberals would have us believe that this wanton destruction—along with the torture and killing of untold thousands of Southern civilians and the bombing of Southern universities, libraries, and hospitals—was necessary in order to "preserve the Union" and "abolish slavery." This is a view that no intelligent person will ever accept.

You have witnessed the illegal theft of farms and plantations, after which they were simply given to Yankee industrialists—in the process creating millions of homeless Southern refugees among all races. You have seen Southern schools, universities, businesses, courthouses, libraries, and even hospitals put to the torch and entire towns bombed into rubble.

All for what? To "preserve the Union"? To "abolish slavery"? The idea is preposterous and an insult to all intelligent people!

Following the end of this nightmare (at Appomattox on April 9, 1865), how would you have reacted to another Yankee onslaught, a second terrorist attack on your loved ones, your home, your land, your town, your rights, your very principles and traditions—a second wave of violence even more spiteful, cruel, unnecessary, and unjustifiable than the first, and which lasted three times longer?

The truth is that having not lived through this terrible period in American history ourselves, we can only imagine, not fully appreciate, what occurred. That is the purpose of the following descriptions, many of them firsthand.

WILLIAM J. SIMMONS ON RECONSTRUCTION & THE KKK

Let us begin our exploration into the foundations of Reconstruction with Colonel William Joseph Simmons of Alabama, founder of the modern KKK in Atlanta, Georgia, in 1915. Simmons provides one of the best and most detailed descriptions of the events leading up to Reconstruction, as well as its impact on Dixie:

> After the Confederate soldiers had laid down their arms and accepted their paroles in good faith, singly, in squads, many of them on foot, without a dollar in their pockets, they returned to their desolate homes and began anew to rebuild their vanished fortunes.
>
> In so far as the Confederate soldier was concerned the war was over; he had fought to the limit of his capacity for the cause he was convinced was right; the issue had been settled by the sword and he had accepted the decree. The reins of government had again been placed in the hands of the best men of the South and the voices of the former army commanders again were heard in the halls of the National Congress. Little attention was paid by them to the mouthings of the [Liberal Yankee] "bloodhounds of hate," directed by Lust and Greed, who, in peacetime, still refused to leave the track of their infamous conquest for spoils.
>
> For over a year peace ostensibly was hovering over the

still smouldering battlefields of the South, but soon the thunder of the impending storm of Reconstruction was heard in the land. Throughout the North, and especially in New England, meetings were held and from pulpits, rostrums and public halls enemies of the South preached *a crusade of extermination against the Southern people*.

William Joseph Simmons, founder and Imperial Wizard of the "New KKK" at Atlanta, Georgia, in 1915. Although Simmons was not correct in drawing a comparison between the Reconstruction KKK and his modern version, the Knights of the Ku Klux Klan, his knowledge of the Reconstruction period and the reasons for the emergence of the first KKK is historically accurate.

If [Union General Ulysses S.] Grant's order to [Union General Henry W.] Halleck to "eat out Virginia clear and clean so that crows flying over it will have, for the balance of the season, to carry their provender with them," or his order to [Union General Philip H.] Sheridan to hang without trial any of

[Confederate Colonel John S.] Mosby's men who were caught, may be excused on the grounds that they were justified by the exigencies of war, what excuse is to be made for this tirade delivered after the war was over by Wendell Phillips from the pulpit of Henry Ward Beecher's church:

> "I do not believe in battles ending this war. You may plant a fort in every district of the South, you make take possession of her capitals and hold them with your armies, but you have not begun to subdue her people. I know it means something like *absolute barbarian conquest*, I allow it, but *I do not believe there will be any peace until 347,000 men of the South are either hanged or exiled.*"

South-hater and Radical New England Liberal Wendell Phillips of Boston, Massachusetts.

And this, some time later, from "Parson" [William G.] Brownlow at a convention held in New York:

> "If I had the power I would arm every wolf, panther, catamount and bear in the

mountains of America, every crocodile in the swamps of Florida, every negro in the South, every devil in hell, clothe them in the uniform of the Federal army and turn them loose on the rebels of the South and *exterminate every man, woman and child south of Mason and Dixon's line*. I would like to see negro troops, under the command of [Union General Benjamin F.] Butler, crowd every rebel into the Gulf of Mexico and *drown them* as the devil did the hogs in the Sea of Galilee."

Like many other Liberal Yanks, Richard Yates, governor of Illinois, wanted the North to continue its war on the Conservative South even after Lee's surrender. It was just such Yankee arrogance that gave birth to the Reconstruction Ku Klux Klan.

In another' convention held in Philadelphia "Parson" Brownlow said:

"I am one of those who believe the [Civil] war ended too soon. *We have whipped the South, but not enough*. The loyal masses constitute an overwhelming majority of the people of this country and they intend to march again on the South and intend this second war shall be no child's play. The second army will, as they ought to, make the entire South as God found the earth—without form and void."

Following Brownlow's speech Governor [Richard] Yates, of Illinois, rose in his seat and said:

"Illinois furnished 250,000 troops to fight the South, and now we are ready to furnish 500,000 more to finish the good work."

Union General Benjamin F. Butler was not nicknamed "the Beast" by Southerners for nothing. This fiendish Yankee war criminal was responsible for scores of outrages against the Southern people, including trying to incite Louisiana blacks to kill their white friends and neighbors.

And who was this Butler that "Parson" Brownlow wished to command an army of negro troops and drive every former Confederate soldier into the Gulf of Mexico? It was [Union General Benjamin F. "the Beast"] Butler who ordered [Union] General [Godfrey] Weitzel to compel the negroes of La Fourche

Parish, Louisiana, to murder the white people of the parish. In reply to this order General Weitzel wrote:

> "The idea of my inciting a negro insurrection is heartrending. I will resign my command rather than induce negroes to outrage and murder the helpless whites."

Union General Godfrey Weitzel refused to be bullied by Federal brass into starting a race riot in Louisiana for the sole purpose of murdering innocent white civilians. This laudable act alone should earn him a memorial in New Orleans.

Indicating the storm of hate let loose upon the South after the Civil War and for the purpose of disclosing what our histories gloss over—that the people of the South were compelled to fight a second war more terrible than the first to preserve their honor and the land of their birth, the former facts compiled by Lamar Fontaine, C. E., Ph.D., of Lyons, Miss., who lived through that perilous period, are reproduced:

> "Thus it was that for two years after the close of the great war in every hamlet and convention hall in the North thousands of preachers, orators and teachers dinned into the ears of the listening multitudes their fiendish venom until a wild wave of *fanatical, insane New England Puritan hate* swept like an East Indian hurricane over the entire North. . . . The Southern members of the National Congress were as impotent to stay the dark whirlwind of Hate as a cork floating upon the crest of a tidal wave. Then a species of negro insanity raged among the negrophiles of the New England states and it too spread like a prairie fire and took possession of the unthinking masses. Books and pamphlets fell from the New England presses like hail from a passing cloud. Men and women, from pulpit and rostrum, advocated the mixing of the negro and the white races and the establishment of a negro republic in the South after its conquered people had first been destroyed and the land rendered, as Parson Brownlow expressed, 'as God found it, without form and void.'"

Judge Salmon P. Chase, one of Lincoln's cabinet, paid a visit to the South after the surrender. Returning home, he said:

> "I found the whites a worn-out, effete race, without vigor, mental or physical. On the contrary the negroes are alive, alert, full of energy. I predict in 25 years the negroes of the South will be at the head of all affairs, political, religious, the arts and sciences."

Henry Ward Beecher asserted:

> "The negro is superior to the white race. If the latter do not forget their pride of race

and color and amalgamate with the purer and richer blood of the blacks they will die out and wither away in unprolific skinniness."

As do many white Liberals today, New Englander Henry Ward Beecher believed that blacks are superior to whites, and so was racist toward fellow Caucasians, a psychological disorder known as ethnomasochism: gaining pleasure from the hatred of one's own race. Here in the traditional South we believe that, as God's children, all the races are equal. The famed clergyman must have skipped over the biblical passages about "one human family" (e.g., Genesis 3:20; Acts 17:26; Galatians 3:28).

The spread of the anti-Southern sentiment throughout the North forced Congress to act and the Reconstruction Act was the result. Southern senators and representatives were sent back to their homes, the entire civil government of the South was disrupted, and the negro was placed in power in every department, state and national. In support of this Reconstruction Act in Congress, James A. Garfield, later elected President of the United States, said:

"This act set out by laying hands on all the rebel state governments and taking the very breath of life out of them. In the next place it puts a bayonet at the breast of every rebel in the South. In the next it leaves in the hands of Congress utter and absolute power over the people of the South."

The [four] Reconstruction acts of Congress constitute the most appalling tragedy in human history. Elections in the South were carried at the point of the bayonet, white men of the South were forced away from the polls and negroes and conscienceless carpetbaggers from the North, who had been in the South only a few weeks, were allowed to cast ballots and were elected to office. *All in violation of our Constitution and every fundamental principle of Republican government.*

These carpetbaggers and their unscrupulous associates in the North were *not* the valiant soldiers who fought and bled in the battlefields, but, using a modern phrase, they were the cowardly "slackers" of that time, pie-counter politicians and unreasonable and unreasoning fanatics.

Constitutional law was stripped by profane hands of her virtuous vestments; ignorance, lust and hate seized the reins of state; the long-established order of society was disrupted by the sudden elevation to power of a grossly inferior race [meaning, in terms of education], led by fiends in human form, and the very blood of the Caucasian race was threatened with an everlasting contamination [a fear also repeatedly expressed by Lincoln and thousands of other Northerners].

The whole land was fastened in the crushing jaws of a ruthless tyranny enthroned by military despotism; law and order, peace and justice were things of the past and that sacred bulwark of human liberty—the Constitution of the United States of America—was in practice considered a "mere scrap of paper." The originators and perpetrators of this, the darkest epoch in the history of the world, were *not* the good people of the North because they were in ignorance of the real facts of what was being done; *those responsible for this unparalleled reign of ruthless despotism were less than a dozen unscrupulous politicians, prompted by hate and led on in their infamous purpose by graft and greed.*

The chastity of [Southern] wife, mother, daughter and

sister was imperiled; life and living were made intolerable. In the name of the Law the property of the [Southern] husband and father was ruthlessly snatched from him without provocation and confiscated and the grim visages of Want, Hunger, Fear and Woe unutterable were visible everywhere.

The people of the South turned appealingly to the power of their national government, but were spurned away with contempt and scorn.

James R. Crowe, one of the six founders of the Reconstruction KKK in late 1865.

But the cry of that defenseless, terrorized and bleeding people, scorned by their own government to which they had sworn renewed allegiance and by which they had been guaranteed protection, and with the treaty of peace signed by Grant and [Robert E.] Lee branded by [Thaddeus] Stevens, in conduct if not in words, as a "scrap of paper," was not to go unanswered.

The men who for four years had borne upon their bayonets the Ark of the Confederacy through one of the most savage wars in all history, heard and answered the cry, and, as Knights of the Invisible Empire, impelled by an instinct of the race, they leaped into the saddle, consecrated to their task by the touch of the hot tears of defenseless womanhood and borne upon the backs of their faithful steeds, they came—they came, they saw, they conquered!

From over the mysterious borderland, from the Empire of the Soul, the Ku Klux came. Out of the sable shadows of the darkest night that ever afflicted any people they rode with a determined purpose; pure, as typified by the snowy white of their ghostly garments; hearts loyal as ever pulsated, as typified by the cross on the crimson shield worn upon their manly breasts; and a sacred devotion that laughed at death and faltered not at danger, as typified by the sacrificial cross of the Christ.

With the fiery cross, symbol of the purest and most loyal patriotism, as their beacon, the Ku Klux rode forth in the cause of humanity, to save . . . [and] restore civilization, protect the defenseless, shield that which was sacred, avenge the crimes against the innocent and to restore to a free-born people their sacred birthright created for them by the shed blood of a noble ancestry.

Through the darkness of Reconstruction's night the Ku Klux rode, dispelled the darkness of that frightful night, and at the dawning of a glorious day they saw the shades of that frightful night receding. Right had been by them established over Might; the voice of music was heard again in the land, their purpose and mission were ended, they laid aside their spotless robes and the noblest order of real chivalry in the great world's history disbanded—the Ku Klux of yesterday rode no more.

In spite of *the noble purpose of the Ku Klux Klan and in spite of the great service it rendered to both the white and the negro races, to North as well as South, yes, to all America, no organization in the history of man ever had heaped upon it the abuse and misrepresentation that fell to its lot.* Foes of the South and enemies of the Southern people viciously assailed it as a band of murderers who stopped at nothing, and who whipped and terrorized both black and white and vented its spite and avenged personal wrongs, real or fancied, upon whoever incurred its displeasure.

No fouler slander ever was perpetrated. Instead of being murderers and cutthroats the members of the Ku Klux Klan were men of the highest type as a body and they were sworn to and stood firmly upon the sacred principles of constitutional law. They worked to safeguard life and property, or what there was left of it; to ameliorate the terrible conditions growing out of the presence of the carpetbaggers from the

North and the scalawags from the South, who turned traitor to their own people, and their baneful influence over the negro.

The Ku Klux of the Reconstruction period was the outgrowth of a dire necessity born of insufferable conditions forced on the Southern people by a group of greedy, conscienceless politicians, and the character of the men who were at its head in the various Southern states is a lasting rebuke to the charge that it was composed of a band of outlaws.

U.S. Secretary of the Treasury and Chief Justice under Lincoln, Salmon Portland Chase of New Hampshire was a typical big government Liberal who helped set up a national bank and the IRS, both unconstitutional. After the War the South-hater was a major player in the Reconstruction process, presiding over the trial to remove pro-South U.S. President Andrew Johnson, and the Leftist campaign to make secession illegal. His belief that blacks are superior to whites (which contradicted Lincoln's view that whites are superior to blacks) upset even his own Yankee constituents and prevented him from becoming U.S. president, one of his lifelong political goals.

Contrary to popular opinion the Ku Klux Klan was not sectional except as to territory. Among its members were many men who had fought in the Federal army and who had decided to make their homes in the South after the war. They held no resentment against their Southern brothers, they realized the insanity of attempting to force negro domination upon the South and they cast their lot with their former foes of the battlefield in the movement to restore the South to its rightful place in the nation.

In addition to these many of the white soldiers of the Federal army of occupation who were actually on duty in the South and who were under orders to kill a member of the Invisible Empire on sight, were members of the Ku Klux Klan. And connected with the Klan work were hundreds of negroes who rendered a service of imperishable value and who suffered torture, and many death, at the hands of the Union League and the carpetbaggers for their unshakable fidelity.

We have said that *the Ku Klux spirit throughout the ages has been the antithesis of tyranny, the foe of despotism, and always has fostered liberty.* Why should we call it the Ku Klux spirit rather than by any other name, and why should we feel warranted in the assertion that it is the antithesis of tyranny?

The answer is found in the fact that men—especially men of the Anglo-Saxon race—have never submitted passively to oppression; his is an unconquered and unconquerable race. No matter how firmly the yoke was fixed about his neck, no matter how sharp was the cut of the lash upon his back, no matter how remote were his chances of securing his liberty, sooner or later he always has rebelled. Sooner or later his hands were at the throat of the tyrant and even though he failed and death was his portion he has died gladly rather than purchase life at the price of chains and slavery. *Tyranny of the most heartless type, despotism of the most devilish nature and to the highest and most powerful degree were established upon the ruined South. Never before was there such conscienceless conduct towards any people.* The people of the South were of and belonged to that "unconquered race." *In the Reconstruction period tyranny reached its greatest height, and to successfully combat it in the interest of the blood-bought human rights of a sovereign people, that spirit which through the ages has always stood—"the antithesis of tyranny"—as at other times, asserted itself as never before. It flamed in human breasts, men united in organized form, an instrument of salvation, and the body, vitalized by this spirit, was called the Ku Klux Klan.*

Wherever and whenever oppression has prevailed that

spirit of resentment, of determination to resist until the shackles are broken always has been found. So has it been always, is today and will be forever.

Sometimes it has smouldered in secret for years and then flashed up at the psychological moment to ignite a world. *Call it by whatever name you will, the spirit of rebellion against tyranny—the spirit of the followers of [John] Calvin and [Martin] Luther and [Oliver] Cromwell, of the Revolutionary fathers, of the Ku Klux of the Reconstruction period—is indestructible, and the man in whose breast that spirit lives will never submit to domination, social, religious or political, by any man or race of men, and will never acquiesce in the rule of injustice or a reign of wrong.*

The Ku Klux spirit has never manifested itself with force except when driven to it by the usurpation of power or attempt to usurp it. *It has never questioned the right of any man of any race to live his life and conduct his own affairs as he sees fit so long as such conduct does not conflict with the established order of society.*[157]

S. E. F. ROSE ON RECONSTRUCTION & THE KKK

Southern historian Mrs. S. E. F. Rose begins her description of Reconstruction shortly after the close of Lincoln's War:

Complete submission was given to the authority of the United States Government by all, those in official and private station as well. Notwithstanding this, Jefferson Davis, President of the Confederate States, was thrust into prison; other leaders of the Confederacy and distinguished citizens were arrested, and members of the Confederate Cabinet were forced to become exiles.

The condition of the South was deplorable indeed. Business destroyed, farms gone to wreck, homes laid waste, many of the returning soldiers disabled and broken in health. There was a track of desolation and devastation, without a parallel in history, estimated fully five miles wide, from the Tennessee line through Georgia to Savannah, through South Carolina, by Columbia, to North Carolina, and the desolation in the valley of Virginia, if possible, was greater.

No money, no stock to work the ground, and nothing at hand with which to begin life again, so it seemed. Four million slaves suddenly emancipated, with no realization whatever of the responsibilities that freedom brought.

Many negroes conceived the idea that freedom meant

cessation from labor, so they left the fields, crowding into the cities and towns, expecting to be fed by the United States Government [thus Lincoln was the founder of America's "nanny state"].[158] So agriculture the chief means of support in the South, was at a standstill. Railroads and other means of transportation were almost wrecked, and chaos reigned supreme.

As part of Reconstruction, Confederate President Jefferson Davis (posing here with his family at his Mississippi home, Beauvoir, around 1884) was illegally arrested and imprisoned. After nearly dying in jail from harsh conditions, cruel treatment, and various health problems, the U.S. government released Davis because it could not find an attorney to prosecute him for "treason." Why? It was well-known that secession was legal in 1861, just as it is today, and no Yankee lawyer believed the government could win such a case against the erudite, highly educated Southerner—who also happened to be extremely well versed in constitutional law.

To the general confusion was added a flood of adventurers from the North, called Carpet-baggers, who were not generally Northern soldiers; but mere camp followers of the Northern armies; men imbued with passions of the lowest order, settling in the South for the purpose of controlling the Southern States by becoming leaders of the negro voters, the best class of white people being excluded from voting by the Reconstruction measures of Congress.

These men hated everything that bore the name "Southern," and at once began to inflame the negroes against their former masters. They were told by these unprincipled men that the Southern people expected to put them back into slavery, and the United States Government was going to give every able-bodied negro man "Forty acres of land and a mule."

In this demoralized state of affairs, in many instances, *private property was seized, and taken possession of in the name of the United States Government.* This was the situation, in 1865, at the South, exhausted, prostrated, disarmed, "overpowered, but not degraded."

And yet Hope remained, for many of those brave heroes,—the Confederate Soldiers—who endured all the hardships of those four terrible years of war, were still left to protect, with their last drop of blood, their beloved Southland.

These conditions, as described in the above lines, at the close of the War between the States, called into existence the Ku Klux Klan, and this organization proved the solution of a problem that confronted the South during the dark days of Reconstruction, and relieved a situation fraught with more terrors than the war itself.

The South was soon under what is known as the Carpet-Bag Regime; men without principle were in power, and negroes, already demoralized by their freedom, were elevated to the highest positions.

The Black and Tan Government, composed of Republican [that is, Liberal] Carpet-baggers, home-made Yankees, or Scalawags, and ignorant and brutal negroes, now held full sway.

Union Leagues, whose members were mainly negroes, and the lowest element of whites, were hotbeds for engendering race strife, and negro equality and plans to place the "black heels on the white necks." Orders from the Freedman's Bureaus were carried out by negro militia. In addition, there were the home Yankees, despicable traitors to the South, who were ready for any deed, no matter how dark, to curry favor with those in power. *The white men of the South were not allowed to vote or carry firearms, and no indignity was too great to be offered them, or their families.*

The negro considered freedom synonymous with equality and his-greatest ambition was to marry a white wife.

Under such conditions the negro clothed with all authority and outnumbering the white, two to one, open resistance would have meant instant death, or being sent to some Northern dungeon, there to languish and die, leaving loved ones exposed to dangers to terrible to contemplate, at the hands of these brutish despots. *Under such conditions there was only one recourse left, to organize a powerful Secret Order to accomplish what could not be done in the open. So the Confederate soldiers, as members of the Ku Klux Klan, and fully equal to any emergency, came again to the rescue, and delivered the South from a bondage worse than death.*[159]

This old illustration of a Reconstruction Klansman is entitled "A Mysterious Messenger."

As Mrs. Rose intimates, surely if there was ever a time for a loyal Southern body of "regulators" to protect the people and their property and maintain the peace, it was now.[160] Even the U.S. Congress would later accept the creation of the original KKK as a logical and understandable Southern reaction to the North's horrid Reconstruction laws, official ineptitude, and general immorality in its dealings with the

South at the time.[161]

WINFIELD JONES ON RECONSTRUCTION & THE KKK
Yankee journalist Winfield Jones described the postwar state of affairs this way. The First Freedmen's Bureau Bill,[162] passed by the U.S. Congress on March 3, 1865, even before the War was over,

> gave [the U.S. government and military] complete jurisdiction over practically everything pertaining to the recently freed slaves. It provided for the employment of agents in all the southern counties, who might be either from civil life or from the army, and who had all the autocratic powers of military judges. The measure abolished ordinary processes of law, set aside the right of *habeas corpus*, destroyed the right of trial by jury, as well as the right of appeal from sentences. This law gave the Federal agents of the Freedmen's Bureau, who were soon swarming in every part of the South, more tyrannical and autocratic powers than were ever possessed by any Romanoff tyrant or Roman consul. *Under the bill, an agent of the Freedmen's Bureau, backed by Federal bayonets, had for a time practically unlimited power over life and property in any county in the South where he set up his authority.*
>
> The Freedmen's Bureau Act was followed by three other measures in the 1866 Congress, all providing for "more efficient government of the rebel states." All of these measures were passed over President [Andrew] Johnson's veto, and the conflict between the Executive and Congress grew more bitter day by day. The measures [along with the four Reconstruction Acts] divided ten of the Southern States into five military districts, each in charge of an army officer who was endowed with absolute and arbitrary powers such as had hardly existed before in any country. President Johnson bitterly denounced these bills and flayed Congress in his veto messages. Naturally the breach between the President and Congress grew wider.
>
> It cannot be denied that *the bestowal of such tyrannical power upon military satraps in the South led to grave abuses in that section. Immense stealings and graft of all kinds, tyrannies, and persecutions of the defeated population occurred which finally culminated in a saturnalia of misgovernment which has hardly been paralleled in history.* This condition afterwards was well recognized in the North and by former Union soldiers. Some

Republican [then the Liberal Party] members of Congress were among the chief opponents of this policy.

Under these laws all men who had served in the Confederate Army, or aided in any way the Confederate States, were disfranchised and could not hold any state or Federal office. This condition continued almost universally in the South until 1872. The result was that the Southern white man had nothing whatever to say concerning his State or the Federal Government. He was governed by a horde of "carpetbaggers" and scalawags of various kinds who invaded the South in large numbers after Appomattox and after the Federal armies were largely disbanded. With the Caucasian race disfranchised, negro rule, led and directed by the white carpetbaggers from the North, followed as a matter of course.

The legislation provided that the five military districts into which the ten Southern States were organized should continue until these States held conventions and adopted new constitutions satisfactory to Congress. It was also required that their legislatures adopt the [openly anti-South] Fourteenth Amendment to the Constitution, and arbitrary rule was to continue until the Fourteenth Amendment had been adopted by three-fourths of the States of the Union.

[Though the requirement of three-fourths of the states was never reached, under] . . . the urging of Senator Charles Sumner, of Massachusetts, the Civil Rights Bill was then passed [illegally *forced* through, would be the more correct term].[163] This law authorized the Federal courts to compel admission of negroes to all public places, and made mandatory that negroes should serve on juries the same as whites. In 1883 the United States Supreme Court held the Civil Rights Law unconstitutional.

Republican [that is, Liberal] members of Congress, who were responsible for the subjection under which the conquered Southern States groaned, set up the contention that conditions in the South required martial law. It is now generally realized in this enlightened age that such a procedure was unwarranted by conditions, and was largely the result of the bitter passions caused by the four years' struggle between the States. The American Constitution provides that a writ of habeas corpus *shall not be suspended except in cases of rebellion or invasion.* Every fairminded man, after the lapse of the past half century, when the hatreds of the great war have been abated or been stilled, must acknowledge there was no excuse for claiming after the war ended that a state of rebellion existed in the South when the Confederate armies had surrendered and disbanded. Certainly there was no invasion of the

South, but the right of habeas corpus was completely nullified by the military agents who governed the South with iron hands.

Most constitutional lawyers will acknowledge now that the reconstruction laws were unconstitutional, as well as wrong and vicious. Their application in the South held back the economic recovery of the Southern States for many years. With the perspective of fifty years behind us we now see that these laws were wrong. Under these statutes practically the entire white population of the South was disfranchised. The former slaves, only a few of whom could read or write, constituted the entire electorate. The carpetbaggers, some of whom were the scum of the earth, led this motley array of negroes and worked their will with them politically, at the same time that they plundered the white population of the South. It was not long before an era of oppression and corruption was in full swing that would have put to shame the most deplorable conditions in the history of any conquered country. So bad was the misgovernment in the South, and so corrupt the conditions prevailing under carpetbag rule, that many of the northern papers of that period printed scathing editorials against the agents of the Freedmen's Bureau and the Southern military government.

To his credit, pro-South Conservative U.S. President Andrew Johnson fought both the North's harsh Reconstruction measures and the Radical Liberals who created them—but to no avail. After narrowly winning his impeachment trial, Johnson continued battling an anti-South Congress right up until progressive Yank Ulysses S. Grant took over his job in 1869.

While the carpetbaggers and rascals of various kinds were misgoverning the South and plundering it, a few good men from the Northern States had immigrated to the South, and these men, many of them former Federal soldiers and officers, unhesitatingly took the part of the oppressed population. Their voices were continually heard in protest through communications to northern newspapers, concerning the saturnalia, of robbery and misgovernment in the Southern States.

Veterans of the Federal armies and the Confederate armies in any Southern community in the United States, who are still alive, will personally corroborate these statements, which do not begin to describe the terrible governmental conditions existing in the South for many years after the end of the Civil War.

In fact, the South was rapidly being reduced to a state of complete ruin by misgovernment of the carpetbaggers and their ignorant negro followers. The freed slaves, as a class, were good people. They had been, except in few cases, well treated and well taken care of by their owners, but in the mass they were illiterate, ignorant, and superstitious, with a leavening of viciousness. They were as putty in the hands of their white [Liberal] leaders. It followed that the government of the Southern States, under such conditions, was undoubtedly one of the worst ever experienced in the history of the world.

. . . As an illustration of the type of carpetbag and ignorant legislators during reconstruction days in the South, the South Carolina State Legislature of 1868-1872 contained 155 members. With hardly an exception they were either negroes or the lowest possible type of whites, and included a large number of carpetbaggers.

Twenty-two members could not read or write. Several were able to only write their names, and 41 signed official documents with an X-mark. Ninety-eight of the 155 members were negroes, and of this number 67 paid no taxes. None of the state officers, with the sole exception of the lieutenant governor, paid any taxes.

Negro militia companies were organized everywhere, and these were used as an instrument by agents of the Freedmen's Bureau and the military government to terrorize the people. The white men were not allowed to join the militia organizations and, whenever possible, they were deprived of arms. The agents of the Freedmen's Bureau and the military judges were bitterly prejudiced against the white population, favorably inclined to the negro, and as many of these officials were themselves ignorant, vicious, and of the lowest type there was practically no justice obtainable by the white man. Federal troops and the negro militia companies were quartered in the cities and towns and were the chief instruments to enforce the authority of the Freedmen's Bureau agents. White men and women were frequently arrested at the caprice of these agents and imprisoned for long periods without being brought before a court. The military commanders in the five zones sometimes interfered at will with the civil courts, and procedure of civil law was subject at any time to the whim of the Freedmen's Bureau agent or a military commander. In some cities civil officers were arbitrarily removed by military commanders, citizens were forbidden to assemble at any time, and even the highest judicial officers of a State Supreme Court were awed or menaced by armed men. A Louisiana Governor was summarily removed by order of a military commander. Military commanders on more than one occasion resisted [Southern] court decrees and forced judges to revoke sentences of their courts. Criminals were forcibly taken from peace officers by negro militia officers and set free. The [Southern] white man was an object of insult, and [Southern] women were never safe from the vilest crimes. Newspapers were suppressed and public lectures forbidden. The Federal soldiers, including the negro militia, managed elections and took charge of the ballot boxes. Citizens who had perpetrated no crimes were seized without authority of law and incarcerated in "bull pens" where formerly negro criminals had been confined.

    Of course, among the horde of agents of the Freedmen's Bureau and among the military officers were men of honesty and high character, but they were in the hopeless minority, and while in their jurisdictions comparatively good government prevailed and justice was administered fairly, these were isolated instances. Some of these honest and capable officers, though few in numbers, did not fail to vigorously protest against deplorable conditions in the South whenever they returned to the North, and gradually there began to percolate through the North a feeling that all was not well in the South.

    . . . The South lay prostrate and groaned in her chains. . . . The conditions were deplorable and the white men were desperate. Armed resistance and another rebellion were out of the question, though writers of that period are practically unanimous in the opinion that if the conditions had continued longer without check guerrilla warfare would have begun everywhere in the South. A remedy against carpetbag domination and negro rule had to be found. It was found by the

Southern white man in the secret organization known as the Ku Klux Klan.[164]

As a reminder, this vivid and sympathetic description of Reconstruction in the South was penned by a Northerner.

James Abram Garfield, later to become America's twentieth president, supported the unconstitutional anti-South Reconstruction Acts, which the U.S. Congress began issuing in March 1867.

GEORGE SUMNERS ON RECONSTRUCTION & THE KKK

One particularly interesting eyewitness account comes from an Englishman named George Sumners, who visited the American South during the years 1870 and 1871, in the middle of Reconstruction:

> The white people in the South at the close of the war were alarmed, not so much by the threatened confiscation of their property by the Federal Government, as by more *present dangers of life and property, virtue and honor, arising from the social anarchy around them.* The negroes were disorderly. Many of them would not settle down to labor on any terms, but roamed about with arms in their hands and hunger in their bellies, and the

governing power, with the usual blind determination of a victorious party, was thinking only all the while of every device of suffrage and reconstruction by which the "freedmen" might be strengthened and made, under Northern dictation, the ruling power in the country. *Agitators of the loosest fiber came down among the towns and plantations, and organizing a Union League, held midnight meetings with the negroes in the woods, and went about uttering sentiments which, to say the least, in all circumstances were anti-social and destructive. Crimes and outrages increased. The law, which must be always more or less weak in thinly populated countries, was all but powerless, and the new governments in the South were unable to repress disorders or to spread a general sense of security throughout the community. A real terror reigned for a time, among the white people, and in this situation the Ku Klux started into being. It was one of those secret organizations which spring up in disordered states of society, when the bonds of law and government are all but dissolved, and when no confidence is felt in the regular administration of justice.* But the power with which the Ku Klux moved in many parts of the South, the knowledge it displayed of all that was going on, the fidelity with which its secret was kept, and the complacency with which it was regarded by the general community, gave this mysterious body a prominence and importance seldom attained by such illegal and deplorable associations. *Nearly every respectable man in the Southern States was not only disfranchised, but under fear of arrest or confiscation; the old foundations of authority were utterly razed before any new ones had yet been laid, and in the dark and benighted interval the remains of the Confederate armies—swept, after a long and heroic day of fair fight, from the field—flitted before the eyes of the people in this weird and midnight shape of a "Ku Klux Klan."*¹⁶⁵

ELIZABETH MERIWETHER ON RECONSTRUCTION & THE KKK

Writing under the pseudonym "George Edmonds," pro-South historian Elizabeth Avery Meriwether devoted an entire chapter in one her books to what she called, "The Reconstruction Period—Hate and Cruelty," a few excerpts from which follow:

> *The full horrors of this dreadful period have never been portrayed. God knows the South was hated enough before and during the war, but after the conquest, as she lay disarmed at the feet of her conquerors, wounded almost unto death, the vengeful ferocity of Republicans [then the*

Liberals] *was something to wonder at.* The events of that period deserve a volume to themselves. I shall only say a few words on the subject. Wendell Phillips, insane hater of the South though he was, sometimes had the honesty to speak plainly of his own party [the Liberal Republicans]. Witness the following:

> "The Republican party," said Phillips, "is not inspired with any humane desire to protect the negro. It uses the bloody shirt for office,[166] and once there, only laughs at it. Today our greatest danger is the Republican party. Wolves in sheep's clothing! Hypocrites! I hail their coming defeat, looking forward to it as the dawning of a glorious day."

After becoming U.S. president midway through Reconstruction, Ulysses S. Grant abused his office and trampled the Constitution by giving unlimited powers to Federal officers installed in the prostrate South—with predictable and disastrous results. Yankees may remember Grant as a Civil War hero, but here in Dixie we remember him as presiding over a "reign of terror" (1869-1877) unlike any other in American history.

From early manhood General [Ulysses S.] Grant was afflicted with the drink disease. Phillips said: "Grant can never stand before a bottle of whiskey without falling down." [Union] General [Abram S.] Piatt, in *Memories of the Men Who Saved the Union*, says: "Grant's habit of drink lost us thousands and thousands of patriotic lives. The attempt to conceal this is not only pitiable, but hopeless."

. . . *Yet to this alcohol-soaked man—this man who could not see a bottle of whiskey without falling down—a Republican Congress gave absolute power over the Southern States [when he was elected president of the U.S. in 1868].* There was no escape from any decree issued from Grant's whiskey-soaked brain. He had power to delegate his rule to any man under him. Grant said to the military commanders under him: *"The law makes the district commanders their own interpreters of their power under it."*

This drunken despot wielded absolute and irresponsible power over the unarmed people of the South. A few samples of the methods Grant's sub-despots used will illustrate the South's condition:

> "Headquarters Fourth Military District of Mississippi. Vicksburg, Miss., June 15, 1868. General Order No. 123.
>
> "First.—Major-Gen. Adelbert Ames is appointed Governor of the State of Mississippi, vice Benjamin G. Humphreys, hereby removed.
>
> "Second.—Captain Jasper Myers is appointed Attorney General of the State of Mississippi, vice C. Hooker, hereby removed.
>
> "Third.—The officers appointed above will repair without delay to Jackson, and enter immediately upon the duties of their respective offices. Headquarters Third Military District, Georgia, Alabama and Florida."

> "Atlanta, Ga., January 13, 1868. Charles J. Jenkins, Milledgeville, Ga.
>
> "Sir:—I have no alternative but to remove you from your office, as you will

see by the enclosed order. I do not deem myself called upon to answer the arguments in your letter. George Meade, Major-General Commanding."

John Booker Kennedy, one of the six founders of the Reconstruction KKK in 1865.

No despot ever felt called upon to answer arguments. Force is the only argument despots use or can understand. Mr. John Imes was the Treasurer of Georgia. Meade wrote him as follows:

"Mr. John Imes: Sir:—I am compelled to remove you from office, as you will see I have done by the enclosed order. George Meade, Major-General Commanding."

Grant's sub-despot over South Carolina wrote as follows:

"Headquarters. Charleston, S. C., Oct. 16, 1867. Judge Aldrich has been suspended, and will not be permitted to hold any court in his circuit. See special Order No. 183, of this date. By command of Brevet Major General Edward R. C. Canby."

Union General Edward R. C. Canby was one of Grant's minions, released into the South to inflict further humiliation and damage on the good people of Dixie.

Does the reader want to know how the sub-despots appointed by Grant ruled the people of the South? To this day that rule is referred to as the "horrors of the reconstruction period." *After the [U.S.] military had full possession of all the offices of the civil courts, from the highest down, malignant bullies everywhere in power, a reign of terror set in almost equal to the awful days of the French Revolution. Every day numbers of the best [Southern] citizens arrested on the most frivolous charges, or no charge whatever, hands and feet fettered as felons, dragged hundreds of miles away from homes and friends, were thrown into dungeon cells, in which they lay months or years in solitary confinement unless death ended their suffering. These prisoners were not permitted to see friends, relatives or counselor-at-law. During their long imprisonment, miserably fed, cursed, abused by jailers, tried by [U.S.] military commissioners, many died, many were condemned and sentenced for life to the Dry*

Tortugas—condemned on evidence no court of justice would have received. It was noticed that the military courts seemed to feel special antipathy to young [Southern] men, to beardless boys—sons of the best citizens. The suffering of these youths in prison, their tortures in the Dry Tortugas, they knew would inflict the keenest anguish on the hearts of parents and relatives. The *Montgomery* (Ala.) *Mail*, speaking of the large number of innocent young [Southern] men sent to the Dry Tortugas, thus describes that place of torment:

> "At the Dry Tortugas the prisoners' heads are shaved. They have to labor under a torrid sun upon a sand bank in the midst of the ocean, with balls and chains about their legs. The [Northern] men who command the [Southern] prisoners are amenable to the laws of neither God or man. *Col. Grental, a [Southern] soldier, was tied up by his thumbs, and treated with every species of cruelty and barbarity.* The laws are silent and newspapers dumb. The prisoner who enters the Dry Tortugas leaves liberty, justice, hope, behind him. Large numbers of young Southern men, for any or no offense, in what is called the reconstruction period, are arrested, go through the farce of a drumhead trial, *presided over by men who take a fiendish delight in torturing any Southern man or woman, nearly always found guilty, and sentenced for life to the Dry Tortugas.* The lips of the Alabama journals are pinned together with bayonets. Our hands are fastened in iron cuffs. We dare not speak the whole truth. *If we did our paper would be suppressed, our business ruined, our wives and children brought to want.*"

Neither the despot Grant nor his sub-despots ever forgot the press. Every officer and private in that army of despotism kept a sharp eye on newspapers, and were quick to apply the muzzle if any paper dared make public their evil deeds. Despotism is a noxious plant, which hates the light and flourishes only in dark places. A few samples will show how despots muzzled the press in the South:

On November 15, 1867, a file of [U.S.] soldiers entered the office of the *Vicksburg Times*, arrested the editor, dragged him to jail. McArdle's offense was having reported in the paper a despotic order made by [U.S.] General [Edward O. C.] Ord, and comparing the situation of the South with that of Poland. McArdle was tried by a military commission (always organized to convict) and condemned. Being a man of talent he took an appeal, but all the influence of the military was against him. The case dragged on for years before a final decision, which I have failed to find.

Union General Edward O. C. Ord, another one of the Liberal North's henchmen during Reconstruction, posing with his family in April 1865.

Early on the morning of August 8, 1867, a body of soldiers forced their way into the office of the *Constitutional Eagle*, published at Camden, Ark., seized, carried off and destroyed all the material of the office. [U.S.] Col. C. C. Gilbert, the small despot commanding the Union soldiers at Camden, justified the acts of his men, saying to the editor:

> "An article in your paper unnecessarily exasperated my soldiers. The press may

censure the servants of the people, but the military are not the servants of the people, but their masters. It is a great impertinence for a newspaper in this State to comment on the military under any circumstances."

The comment which unnecessarily exasperated the soldiers was a statement that when drunk the soldiers were in the habit of indecently exposing their persons on the street when ladies were passing. The *National Intelligencer* of Washington City commented on the rule of the military satraps in the South, as follows:

> "Without any proof whatever four respectable [Southern] citizens were arrested and confined in separate cells in Atlanta, denied all communication with friends, save under military surveillance, denied all opportunity to confer with legal counsel. Two white men in Fort Pulaski were confined in cells and denied all access to friends or legal counsel. These six men were brought out of their dungeons, hurried to trial for their lives before a military commission, one of those institutions, Mr. Webster said, always organized to convict. The statement of facts is sufficiently horrible and damnable to every officer and agent concerned in it. But this is only a part of the infamous record. *While these men are immured in dungeons, cut off from all access to friends or counsel, their enemies, with artful and incessant malice, have been busy in procuring false testimony, and the uniform of the nation is degraded by the military arrest of ignorant negroes, dragging them by force before a military board, and then by threats and curses, starvation and solitary confinement, endeavor to extort from them false testimony upon which the lives of innocent men may be taken away.* The testimony we publish to-day establishes these facts, and shows the character of the government under which the people of the

South now live."

These Reconstruction Klansmen from Alabama are not what they appear to be to modern day Liberals: "ruthless thugs and racist mercenaries." In reality, beneath the frightening costumes were average white and black Southern men, most former Confederate soldiers, who used fear not violence as their primary weapon.

These military lords permitted the farce of elections, if carried on under military control. Armed battalions of negroes and Federal white men surrounded the voting places. In vain Democrats [the Conservatives of that day] issued protests against these outrages. In the House of Congress Mr. Brooks, in behalf of the Democratic members, offered a powerful protest.

"The military," said the protest, "have been used to destroy States. The General of the army (Grant), representing the sword, and only the sword (he represented a whiskey bottle also), has been exalted by acts of

Congress above the constitutional Commander in Chief (the President) of the [U.S.] Army and Navy, in order to execute these military decrees and *root out every vestige of constitutional law and liberty*. To prolong and perpetuate this military rule in the North and West, as well as the South, this same General of the army (Grant) has been elected at the Chicago Convention to head the electoral votes for the Presidency in ten States of this Union, which are as much under his feet as Turkey is under the Sultan's, or Poland under the Czar of Russia."

If the protests from Northern Democrats [Conservatives] did not stem the tide of [Yankee] despotism, they at least showed that a spark of the old fire of liberty yet existed in this corrupted Union. *At one stroke of the pen [Union General Philip H.] Sheridan, Grant's sub-despot, disfranchised thirty thousand white men in Louisiana. Grant was responsible for every criminal act done by the military.* The *New York Herald* said of Grant's brutality in the South:

"Every personal right of the citizen is invaded at once. *Without any process of law whatever, a man is deprived of his liberty and thrust into a cell at the mere bidding of a political or military bully.* The secrecy of the telegraph and post office is violated as no man would dare violate them in despotic France."

At that time France was ruled by an Emperor. *The South was ruled by the despotism of hate. No Christian Emperor, King or Kaiser was ever so cruel, so bitter, so vindictive as the hate despotism imposed by Grant upon the people of the South. By bogus elections carpetbaggers went to Congress. It seemed that the chief aim of these bogus Congressmen was to obtain additional power to rob, oppress and torment the people of the South. The excuse for seeking Congressional aid was the ready lie that the people of the South were on the eve of another rebellion.* On the 23rd of July a bill to send more soldiers and munitions of war to the Southern States was up for discussion. A [Liberal scallywag] man by the name of Stokes, who claimed to represent a Tennessee Congressional district, spoke as follows:

> "If you do not send us guns and powder and bayonets and cannon, and send 'em quick, Forrest and his rebel crew of Democrats [Conservatives] will be down on us like—like a thousand devils! I want ten thousand stand of arms for my own district. Unless you send on these arms all the truly loyal negroes will be overrun and the Republican [Liberal] party killed in Tennessee."

The well respected, physically impressive, 6 foot, two inch Forrest, seen here as he appeared during Reconstruction, had a well deserved reputation for his "rough handling" of anti-South partisans. Known by both fellow Confederates and his Yankee foes as the most fearless, formidable, and outstanding cavalry officer in Lincoln's War—one who had killed 30 Yanks with his bare hands—it is little wonder that he ended up serving as the symbolic figurehead of the Reconstruction Klan in the South's second fight against Northern tyranny and oppression.

Mr. Washburn, of Illinois, seemed to be very anxious to send guns and bayonets down to the loyal negroes and carpetbaggers, but he was afraid. "Sir," said Mr. Washburn, "sir, I believe that in most of the States not ten days after these arms are sent South to the loyal negroes they will be in the hands of the rebels."

[The U.S.] Congress saw the danger. Never before was any Congress in so painful a quandary. Anxious, yet afraid, to arm loyal negroes and carpetbaggers. A [Liberal scallywag] man named Dewees, claiming to represent the [largely Conservative] people of North Carolina (he might as well have claimed to represent the people in the moon or the farthest star), added to the distress and perplexity of Congress. "If you don't give us arms," cried Mr. Dewees, pale and anxious, "before six months the Ku-Klux-Klan, the Rebels and the Copperheads will be ruling the whole South."

[Allegedly] Ku-Klux, Rebels and Copperheads were a trinity of devils. Hades had no worse. Still, Congress was afraid to send to the loyal negroes and carpetbaggers munitions of war, which seems a little strange to us of this generation, knowing, as all now know, that the Ku-Klux or Rebels in the South had no arms or munitions of war, while the loyal negroes and carpetbaggers were well armed. A Democrat [Conservative] named Woodward ventured to ask if the reconstruction government in the South could be maintained in no other way than by the bayonet. This question aroused Mr. Dewees' indignation. "No!" he roared. "We can only sustain our Government by arms! Arms we must have, or Ku-Klux, Rebels and Copperheads will wipe us out and rule the South."[167]

WOODROW WILSON ON RECONSTRUCTION & THE KKK

America's twenty-eighth president, Woodrow Wilson, too was well aware of what created the need for a protective society like the KKK. Writing of the Southern people in 1865 and 1866, he made the following observations:

> Adventurers swarmed out of the North to cozen, beguile, and use them. These men, mere "carpet baggers" for the most part, who brought nothing with them, and had nothing to bring, but a change of clothing and their wits, became the new masters of the blacks. They gained the confidence of the negroes, obtained

for themselves the more lucrative offices, and lived upon the public treasury, public contracts, and their easy control of affairs. For the negroes there was nothing but occasional allotments of abandoned or forfeited land, the pay of petty offices, a per diem allowance as members of the conventions and the state legislatures which their new masters made business for, or the wages of servants in the various offices of administration. Their ignorance and credulity made them easy dupes. A petty favor, a slender stipend, a trifling perquisite, a bit of poor land, a piece of money satisfied or silenced them. It was enough, for the rest, to play upon their passions. They were easily taught to hate the men who had once held them in slavery, and to follow blindly the [Northern Liberal] political party which had brought on the war of their emancipation.

U.S. President Woodrow Wilson of Virginia, though a Liberal, understood the climate in which the original KKK emerged and was sympathetic to what the South endured, both during Lincoln's War and during the Reconstruction aftermath. For this he continues to be called a "racist" by fellow ill-informed, uncultivated, and uneducated Liberals.

There were soon lands enough and to spare out of which to make small gifts to them without sacrifice of gain on the part of their new masters. *In Mississippi, before the work of the carpet baggers was done, six hundred and forty thousand acres of land had been forfeited for taxes, twenty per cent, of the total acreage of the State.* The state tax levy for 1871 was four times as great as the levy for 1869 had been; that for 1873 eight times as great; that for 1874 fourteen times. *The impoverished planters could not carry the intolerable burden of taxes, and gave their lands up to be sold by the sheriff. There were few who could buy. The lands lay waste and neglected or were parcelled out at nominal rates among the negroes.* In South Carolina the taxes of 1871 aggregated $2,000,000 as against a total of $400,000 in 1860, though the taxable values of the State were but $184,000,000 in 1871 and had been $490,000,000 in 1860. There were soon lands to be had for the asking wherever the tax gatherer of the new governments had pressed his claims. The assessed valuation of property in the city of New Orleans sank, during the eight years of carpet-bag rule, from $146,718,790 to $88,613,930. Four years and a half of "reconstruction" cost Louisiana $106,020,337. The demoralization of affairs in Louisiana had begun in 1862, when [Yankee] General [Benjamin F.] Butler took possession of the city of New Orleans. The rich spoils of the place had proved too much for the principles of the men intrusted with the management of her affairs in times when law was silent; and the political adventurers who came out of the North to take charge of the new government set up under Mr. [Thaddeus] Stevens's plan of reconstruction found the work they had come to do already begun. *Taxes, of course, did not suffice. Enormous debts were piled up to satisfy the adventurers. The cases of Louisiana and South Carolina were no doubt the worst, but other States suffered in proportion to the opportunities they afforded for safe depredation.* In 1868 the debt of South Carolina had been $5,000,000; in 1872 it was nearly $30,000,000. The debt of Louisiana in 1868 had been between six and seven millions; in 1872 it was $50,000,000. Where the new rulers acted with less assurance and immunity or with smaller resources at hand, debts grew more slowly, but *the methods of spoliation were everywhere much the same; and with the rise of debts went always the disappearance of all assets wherewith to pay them. Treasuries were swept clean. Immense grants were made in aid of public works which were never completed, sometimes not even begun. Railways were subsidized, and the subsidies, by one device or another, converted into outright gifts, which went into the pockets of those who had procured them, not into the building or equipment of the road. A vast burden of debt was piled up for coming generations to carry; the present generation was much too poor to pay anything.

The real figures of the ruin wrought no man could get at. It was not to be expressed in state taxes or state debts. The increase in the expenditure and indebtedness of counties and towns, of school districts and cities, represented an aggregate greater even than that of the ruinous sums which had drained the treasuries and mortgaged the resources of the governments of the States; and men saw with their own eyes what was going on at their own doors. What was afoot at the capitals of their States they only read of in the newspapers or heard retailed in the gossip of the street, but the affairs of their own villages and country-sides they saw corrupted, mismanaged, made base use of under their very eyes. There the negroes themselves were the office holders, men who could not so much as write their names and who knew none of the uses of authority except its insolence. It was there that the policy of the congressional leaders wrought its perfect work of fear, demoralization, disgust, and social revolution.

No one who thought justly or tolerantly could think that this veritable overthrow of civilization in the South had been foreseen or desired by the men who had followed Mr. Stevens and Mr. [Benjamin F.] Wade and Mr. [Oliver P.] Morton in their policy of rule or ruin. That handful of leaders it was, however, hard to acquit of the charge of knowing and intending the ruinous consequences of what they had planned. They would take counsel of moderation neither from northern men nor from southern. They were proof against both fact and reason in their determination to "put the white South under the heel of the black South." They did not know the region with which they were dealing. Northern men who did know it tried to inform them of its character and of the danger and folly of what they were undertaking; but they refused to be informed, did not care to know, were in any case fixed upon the accomplishment of a single object. Their colleagues, their followers, kept, many of them, a cooler mind, a more prudent way of thought, but could not withstand them. They, too, were ignorant of the South. They saw but a little way into the future, had no means of calculating what the effects of these drastic measures would be upon the life and action of the South, and lacked even the knowledge of mere human nature which might have served them instead of an acquaintance with the actual men they were dealing with. *They had not foreseen that to give the suffrage to the negroes and withhold it from the more capable white men would bestow political power, not upon the negroes, but upon white adventurers, as much the enemies of the one race as of the other. In that day of passion, indeed, they had not stopped to speculate what the effects would be. Their object had been to give the negro political power in order that he might defend his own rights, as voters everywhere else might defend theirs. They had not recked of consequences; for a little while they had not cared what they might be.*

They had prepared the way for the ruin of the South, but they had hardly planned to ruin it.

According to President Woodrow Wilson, during Reconstruction this man, Ohio Senator Benjamin F. Wade, engaged in a "policy of rule or ruin" in Dixie, a Northern Liberal attempt to "disintegrate Southern society."

... The price of the policy to which it gave the final touch of permanence was the temporary disintegration of southern society and the utter, apparently the irretrievable, alienation of the South from the political party whose mastery it had been Mr. Stevens's chief aim to perpetuate. *The white men of the South were aroused by the mere instinct of self-preservation to rid themselves, by fair means or foul, of the intolerable burden of governments sustained by the votes of ignorant negroes and conducted in the interest of adventurers: governments whose incredible debts were incurred that thieves might be enriched, whose increasing loans and taxes went to no public use but into the pockets of party managers and corrupt contractors.* There was no place of open action or of constitutional agitation, under the terms of reconstruction, for the men who were the real leaders of the southern communities. Its restrictions shut white men of the older order out from the suffrage [voting] even. *They could act only by private combination, by private means, as a force outside the government, hostile to it, proscribed by it, of whom opposition and bitter resistance was expected, and expected with defiance.* Sober men kept their heads; prudent men saw how sad an increase of passion would come out of hasty counsels of strife, an open grapple between those outlawed and those appointed to govern. Men whom experience had chastened saw that only the slow processes of opinion could mend the unutterable errors of a time like that. But there were men to whom counsels of prudence seemed as ineffectual as they were unpalatable, men who could not sit still and suffer what was now put upon them. *It was folly for them to give rein to their impulses; it was impossible for them to do nothing.*

They took the law into their own hands, and began to attempt by intimidation what they were not allowed to attempt by the ballot or by any ordered course of public action. They began to do by secret concert and association what they could not do in avowed parties. Almost by accident a way was found to succeed which led insensibly farther and farther afield into the ways of violence and outlawry. In May, 1866, a little group of young men in the Tennessee village of Pulaski, finding time hang heavy on their hands after the excitements of the field, so lately abandoned, *formed a secret club for the mere pleasure of association, for private amusement,*—for anything that might promise to break the monotony of the too quiet place, as their wits might work upon the matter, and one of their number suggested that they call themselves the *Kuklos*, the Circle. Secrecy and mystery were at the heart of the pranks they planned: secrecy with regard to the membership of their Circle, secrecy with regard to the place and the objects of its meetings; and the mystery of disguise and of silent parade when the comrades rode abroad at night when the moon was up: a white mask, a tall cardboard hat, the figures of man and horse sheeted like a ghost, and the horses' feet muffled to move without sound of their approach. It was the delightful discovery of the thrill of awesome fear, the woeful looking for of calamity that swept through the countrysides as they moved from place to place upon their silent visitations, coming no man could say whence, going upon no man knew what errand, that put thought of mischief into the minds of the frolicking comrades. It threw the negroes into a very ecstasy of panic to see these sheeted "Ku Klux" move near them in the shrouded night; and their comic fear stimulated the lads who excited it to many an extravagant prank and mummery. No one knew or could discover who the masked players were; no one could say whether they meant serious or only innocent mischief; and the zest of the business lay in keeping the secret close.

In the opinion of President Wilson, Indiana Governor Oliver P. Morton, shown here around 1875, was one of those who sought to destroy Dixie by "putting the white South under the heel of the black South." Thus to Morton and thousands like him must be laid the responsibility for the many horrors of Reconstruction.

Here was a very tempting and dangerous instrument of power for days of disorder and social upheaval, when law seemed set aside by the very government itself, and outsiders, adventurers, were in the seats of authority, the poor negroes, and white men without honor, their only partisans. Year by year the organization spread, from county to county, from State to State. Every country-side wished to have its own Ku Klux, founded in secrecy and mystery like the mother "Den" at Pulaski, until at last there had sprung into existence a great Ku Klux Klan, an "Invisible Empire of the South," bound together in loose organization to protect the southern country from some of the ugliest hazards of a time of revolution. The objects of the mysterious brotherhood grew serious fast enough. It passed from jest to earnest. Men took hold of it who rejoiced to find in it a new instrument of political power: men half outlawed, denied the suffrage, without hope of justice in the courts, who meant to take this means to make their will felt. "They were to protect their people from indignities and wrongs; to succor the suffering, particularly the families of dead confederate soldiers"; to enforce what they conceived to be the real laws of their States "and defend the constitution of the United States and all laws passed in conformity thereto; to aid in executing all constitutional laws and protect the people from unlawful seizures and from trial otherwise than by jury." Similar secret orders grew up alongside the great Klan, or in States where its "dens" had not been established: Knights of the White Camellia, Pale Faces, Constitutional Union Guards, the White Brotherhood, to serve the same ends by the same means. The Knights of the White Camellia, founded in New Orleans in the winter of 1867-1868, spread their organization abroad more widely even than the Ku Klux Klan.

It was impossible to keep such a power in hand. Sober men governed the counsels and moderated the plans of these roving knights errant; but it was lawless work at best. *They had set themselves, after the first year or two of mere mischievous frolic had passed, to right a disordered society through the power of fear.* Men of hot passions who could not always be restrained carried their plans into effect. Reckless men not of their order [imposters], malicious fellows of the baser sort who did not feel the compulsions of honor and who had private grudges to satisfy, imitated their disguises and borrowed their methods. What was done passed beyond mere mummery, mere visiting the glimpses of the moon and making night hideous, that they might cause mere "fools of nature horridly to shake their disposition with thoughts beyond the reaches of their souls." *It became the chief object of the night-riding comrades to silence or drive from the country the principal mischief-makers of the [Northern Liberal] reconstruction regime, whether white or black.* The negroes were generally easy enough to deal with: a thorough fright usually disposed them to make utter submission, resign their parts in affairs, leave the country,—do anything their ghostly visitors demanded. But white men were less tractable; and here and there even a negro ignored or defied them. The regulators would not always threaten and never execute their threats. They backed their commands, when need arose, with violence. Houses were surrounded in the night and burned, and the inmates shot as they fled, as in the dreadful days of border warfare. Men were dragged from their houses and tarred and feathered. Some who defied the vigilant visitors came mysteriously to some sudden death.

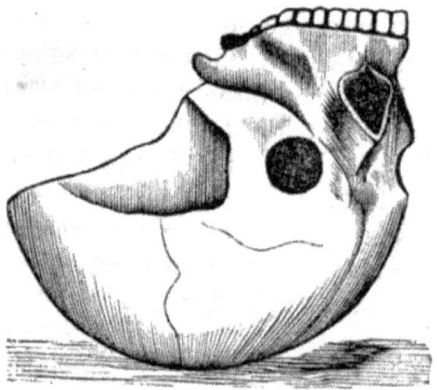

"The Consecrating Bowl," another piece of the bizarre paraphernalia of the Reconstruction KKK, meant to instill panic and dread in white and black carpetbaggers and scallywags.

The more ardent regulators made no nice discriminations. All northern white men or women who came into the South to work among the negroes, though they were but school teachers, were in danger of their enmity and silent onset. Many of the teachers who worked among the negroes did in fact do mischief as deep as any political adventurer. The lessons taught in their schools seemed to be lessons of self-assertion against the whites: they seemed too often to train their pupils to be aggressive Republican [that is, Liberal] politicians and mischief-makers between the races. The innocent and enlightened among them suffered in the general opinion from the errors of those who deliberately sowed discord; and the regulators too often failed to discriminate between those who made trouble and those who fulfilled their gentle errand in peace and good temper.

The ranks of those who flocked into the South to take part in the reconstruction of the States and the habilitation of the negro for his life of freedom were strangely mixed of good and bad. The teachers came upon an errand of mercy and humanity, but came *too many of them with bitter thoughts and intolerant purpose against the white people of the South, upon whom, as they did not reflect, the fortunes of the negro in any case depended. The politicians came for the most part like a predatory horde*; but here and there emerged a man of integrity, of principle, of wise and moderate counsel, who in the long run won the confidence even of those who hated with an ineradicable hatred the [Liberal] party and the practice of [Northern] federal control which he represented. *The Ku Klux and those who masqueraded in their guise struck at first only at those who made palpable mischief between the races or set just law aside to make themselves masters*; but their work grew under their hands, and their zest for it. Brutal crimes were committed; the innocent suffered with the guilty; a reign of terror was brought on, and society was infinitely more disturbed than defended. Law seemed oftentimes given over. The right to the writ of *habeas corpus* was again and again suspended to check the lawless work. At least one governor of the reconstruction period sent to his adjutant general lists of leading citizens proscribed, with the suggestion that those whose names were specially marked should be tried by court martial and executed at once before the use of the writ should be restored. One lawless force seemed in contest with another.

Such was the disturbing subject matter of the news which crept north during the first year of General [Ulysses S.] Grant's administration as President.[168]

THOMAS NELSON PAGE ON RECONSTRUCTION & THE KKK
President Wilson's ambassador to Italy, Southern writer and attorney Thomas Nelson Page, asserted that:

The war between the states destroyed the institution of slavery, the dark years of the carpetbagger's domination well-nigh destroyed the South and Anglo-Saxon civilization, for after the sword came the canker worm and the enforcement of despotic intrigue.[169]

Thomas Nelson Page, President Wilson's Italian ambassador, correctly referred to Reconstruction as "the canker worm and the enforcement of despotic intrigue."

ANNIE C. BURTON ON RECONSTRUCTION & THE KKK

Annie Cooper Burton, a member of the United Daughters of the Confederacy, wrote the following in 1916:

> The great Ku Klux Klan sprang up like a mushroom, a Southern organization formed in a time when no other power in the world could have saved the suffering South from the utter disorder which prevailed during the awful period following the War between the States.
>
> The stigma attached to the name Ku Klux Klan by the uninformed masses has, at this late day, been practically

removed, thanks to that Southern author, Thomas J. Dixon [Jr.], who through [his novel] *The Clansman* swayed public opinion the right way; and thanks again to that master director, David W. Griffith, another Southerner, who filmed this wonderful story and set the people to exclaiming, *"Why, the Ku Klux Klan was a grand and noble order! It ranks with the best."*

Every clubhouse of the United Daughters of the Confederacy should have a memorial tablet dedicated to the Ku Klux Klan; that would be a monument not to one man, but to five hundred and fifty thousand men, to whom all Southerners owe a debt of gratitude; for how our beloved Southland could have survived that reign of terror is a big question.

The very name Ku Klux shows that the order was formed among men of letters. It is a Greek word meaning circle. Klan suggested itself; the name complete in turn suggested mystery. Originally the order was purely a social organization, formed in Pulaski, Tennessee, May, 1866, and gave diversion to the restless young men after the reaction of war. They found vast amusement in belonging to a club which excited and baffled curiosity; great sport, too, was found in initiating new members. But *it was when the Klan realized that it had a great, vital work to perform that it rose majestically to the gigantic task.*

When the order at the end of a year had grown throughout the South to such a size that *a master hand was needed to guide it, Nathan Bedford Forrest*, famous cavalry general of the Southern Army, he of the charmed life, a man who was in "more than one hundred battles and had twenty-seven horses shot under him," a leader famous for his military strategy, was [brought in to help guide] . . . the Invisible Empire. *Forrest always stressed the order that no fighting would be allowed. If they needed to fight they would throw off their disguise and fight like soldiers. Their purpose was to scare into submission the unruly free negroes and the trouble-making carpetbaggers; and this purpose they accomplished, without one drop of blood being shed, except in the most extreme cases. Whenever an undesirable citizen was not wanted, he generally found a note tacked to his door saying that if he did not move on within twenty-four hours he would be visited by the Ku Klux Klan. Signed "K. K. K." The man generally "moved on" long before the stipulated time.*

The negroes, being naturally superstitious and imaginative, helped the order to gain power. In Nashville, Tennessee, among the five dens, there was one formed of medical students from the University. One of the favorite pranks of these young doctors was to ask a negro to hold their horse, and then place in his hand as he reached out to take the lines a finger or a hand taken from a corpse. The negro generally went a mile before he stopped running. Another effective trick practiced by the Klan was, when they had a negro on trial, to sprinkle beforehand a little powder on the floor—"hell fire," they called it—and when the negro would be looking down at the floor one of the Klansmen would surreptitiously run his foot over the powder line, and a fiery-looking trail would show. The negro would be paralyzed with fright, and was always careful in the future never to have cause to be brought before the Order again.

Thomas Dixon Sr., a member of the Reconstruction Klan and the father of clergyman Thomas Dixon Jr., the author of the 1905 novel *The Clansman*.

The Klan practiced numerous clever devices. Fancy the impression made on a negro when a robed Klansman asked him for a drink of water, to see a whole pail go down without any effort (a rubber bag concealed in the uniform aided in this deception), and then to hear a sepulchral voice say, "This is the first drink I have had since I was killed at Chickamauga!"

One never knew when nor where to expect a body of Ku Klux; they would spring up out of the ground, to all appearances; their ghostly figures multiplying like magic; they had a manner of forming their companies which made a band of one hundred men appear like a thousand. Their horses' feet were always muffled, making their approach completely noiseless. *But it was only the guilty who feared them; and fear was what the Klan worked to effect. To kill was not their aim, and only where absolutely necessary was it ever resorted to.*

Reverend Thomas Dixon Jr., author of *The Clansman*, which inspired David W. Griffith's landmark 1915 Civil War film, *The Birth of a Nation*. Uneducated South-haters continue to call Dixon a racist. But was he? Here is what he had to say on the subject of race in 1896: "I thank God that there is not to-day the clang of a single slave's chain on this continent. Slavery may have had its beneficent effects, but democracy is the destiny of the race, because all men are bound together in the bonds of fraternal equality with one common Father above." Forrest would have wholeheartedly agreed.

The [Reconstruction] Ku Klux Klan lasted for three years; they disbanded as quietly and as quickly as they formed. When martial law was declared, and the work was done, Forrest sent out this order, through word of mouth, from den to den, throughout the vast Empire:

"The Invisible Empire has accomplished the purpose for which it was organized. Civil

> law now affords ample protection to life, liberty and property; robbery and lawlessness are no longer unrebuked; the better elements of society are no longer in dread for the safety of their property, their persons, and their families. The Grand Wizard, being invested with power to determine questions of paramount importance, in the exercise of the power so conferred, now declares the Invisible Empire and all the subdivisions thereof dissolved and disbanded forever."

Uniforms, oaths, and rituals were ordered burned, because it meant death to a Klansman to have them found in his possession, so strong had grown the feeling against the Order, due to unscrupulous outsiders who committed horrible deeds in the guise of the Klan. But the grand old Order had accomplished what it set out to do. *Its work was nobly done; and our rescued South still sings her gratitude to her heaven-sent protectors, the mysterious K. K. K.*[170]

HENRY P. FRY ON RECONSTRUCTION & THE KKK

Owing to the cruelty of the postwar Yankee and the Liberals' ugly attempt to Northernize the South, even many former disgruntled KKK members often empathized with the Klan. In 1922 one of these, Henry Peck Fry, an anti-KKK writer, wrote:

> *The reconstruction of the Southern States following the Civil War was utterly stupid, and Americans of our generation—regardless of Northern or Southern birth—so consider it, and know that the manner in which the situation was handled was a political mistake.*
>
> The activities of the "carpetbaggers" and their negro allies after the Civil War were not confined merely to the looting of the public treasuries. *Vicious white men organized the negroes into societies and stirred up their hatred against the white people, with the result that unspeakable crimes were committed in all parts of the South. Perhaps the most notorious of these [Liberal Northern] organizations was that known as the "Loyal League," which operated in all parts of the South, and which was composed of negroes and low white men.*

... *The agency by which the South was saved from the devilish scheme of Thaddeus Stevens to [Northernize it] ... was the original Ku Klux Klan! Brought into being by chance, and used as an agency to meet the exigency of the hour, it served its purpose as many similar systems have served theirs, including the Western vigilantes, whose work has been commended by Theodore Roosevelt on the ground of public necessity. Then having restored the South to the control of its better element, it passed away, to occupy a cherished place in the history of the Southern States, from which it can never be resurrected.*

Our twenty-sixth president, Liberal-leaning New Yorker Theodore Roosevelt, publicly praised the Western vigilantes, a group that was nearly identical in origins and purpose to the Reconstruction KKK. Why then does the latter continue to be excoriated by the Left?

The reign of Ku Kluxism existed in the Southern States from the year 1866 until President Rutherford B. Hayes withdrew the Federal troops from the South [in 1877, when Reconstruction was officially terminated] ... *[T]he Ku Klux movement was the exercise of extra-legal force for the purpose of meeting a revolutionary condition of society in a revolutionary manner.*

... *The movement was a revolution to meet a situation unparalleled in this country's history*, and the history of revolutions has never at any time manifested the character of pink teas or church socials. Personally I prefer to adopt the point of view that *in a chaotic and despotic condition of society like the one forced upon the Southern people, the end justified the means, and would place the entire responsibility of what happened in the South upon the shoulders of Thaddeus Stevens and other radical [Northern Liberal] leaders of Congress.*[171]

JAMES M. BEARD ON RECONSTRUCTION & THE KKK

In 1877, with the close of Reconstruction that year, historian James Melville Beard wrote poetically of this period, with the memory still fresh in his mind:

> Cities destroyed; towns and villages laid waste; churches, schools, and public buildings rotting under the hospital plague, or, more fortunate, sleeping in the ashes of licensed incendiarism; wealthy plantations stripped of their agricultural paraphernalia, and relegated to the domain whence they had been lately redeemed by the good offices of the pioneer; and in room of these—landscape horrors; vast cemeteries, whose enforced tribute reached unto all kindreds; flame-scarred wastes memorializing a past civilization, and extending from the Alleghany hills to the Georgian forests, and from the rivers to the sea; and brooding over all, sole relic of the conqueror's power, that grim sentinelcy that looked down from dismantled ruins, and bleak, wind-shaken towers, upon the burial-place of the domestic arts.[172]

THE KKK WAS A CONSERVATIVE CONSTITUTIONAL GROUP

From the words of past thinkers, politicians, and writers, we can see how the poisonous environment of anger, fear, terror, oppression, devastation, and frustration created by the Leftist North after Lincoln's War led directly to the formation of the Reconstruction Ku Klux Klan.

The Reconstruction KKK was, in fact, a Conservative Southern response to the second violent intrusion and insistent meddling of the Liberal North. This makes it, in essence, a resurrected version of the Confederate army fighting for the traditional Christian South and the Constitution in the Second American Civil War.

This organizational "response" was pure survival instinct, a desire to preserve and protect the Southern people from harm by a unrelentingly nosy and brutal Yankee neighbor. Protection did not come by way of unlawful acts and crimes, as the North baselessly asserts, but by the KKK binding itself "to allegiance to the laws of the United States" and the Constitution, a strict adherence to law that has always been the hallmark of traditional Conservatism. Indeed, as we have seen, the Reconstruction Klan was "opposed to the shedding of human blood," and its methods were "generally peaceful and without undue destruction to life and property."[173]

A modern Klansman, circa the 1920s. The New KKK has no connection to the Reconstruction KKK, except for the name and some of its apparel—an important fact that is routinely glossed over by the anti-South movement.

Of all those responsible for Reconstruction and its many evils, none was more responsible than history-ignorant busybody and Yankee supremacist Thaddeus Stevens of Vermont. Here was a man who did more to injure the South and her people than anyone else except Lincoln. From creating the malevolent and dangerous anti-white Union Leagues to unlawfully wiping out the South's state governments, Stevens was behind it all. His goal? To "put the white South under the heel of the black South." Only his death from health problems in 1868, shortly after the start of Reconstruction, prevented him from doing more damage, and only the Reconstruction KKK (which he helped inspire) saved the South from the disastrous fallout that came later. How many Southerners were tortured, raped, and murdered as a result of his nefarious actions will never be known. The New Englander's Radical Reconstruction plans included a full scale Northernization of Dixie, right down to eliminating Southern accents! "The whole fabric of Southern society must be changed," he argued, and, according to him, only his revolutionary plan would "work *a radical reorganization in Southern institutions, habits and manners.*" Obsessed with destroying "Southern slavery," like Liberals today he never acknowledged that the "peculiar institution" got its start in his own backyard (Massachusetts), that the American abolition movement was born in the South (Virginia), and that the South was (and always has been) more racially tolerant than the North. Understandably, we traditional Southerners still cringe at Steven's name, maintaining that there is an especially hot place in Hell where he is roasting still.

4

Charges Against Forrest Concerning the KKK

WAS FORREST THE FOUNDER OF THE KKK?

NOW FOR SOME PLAIN SPEAKING. The anti-South movement delights in condemning Forrest for his role as the father and first leader, or Grand Wizard, of the Ku Klux Klan.[174] But in reality neither charge is true.

The names of the six men who established the KKK on Christmas Eve 1865, in a haunted house in Pulaski, Tennessee, are legendary and well-known.[175] They are: J. Calvin Jones, Captain John C. Lester, Richard R. Reed, Captain James R. Crowe, Frank O. McCord, and Captain John B. Kennedy.[176] As we have seen, Forrest did not begin to associate with the organization until two years later, in 1867, the year the Klan held its first public parade.[177] Obviously then he could not have been the founder.

FORREST AS GRAND WIZARD?

As for the General's alleged role as the Grand Wizard of the KKK (the leader of the entire organization),[178] even many among the virulent anti-Forrest movement admit that there is no evidence for this other than hearsay and Yankee folklore,[179] for Klan members never recorded anything on paper,[180] and as such, no official records exist stating that he was their leader.[181] Indeed, no Klansman in Forrest's day ever named the Grand Wizard in public.

John C. Lester, for example, one of the founders of the

organization, wrote a complete history of the original KKK and never named him. Forrest's chief of artillery, John W. Morton, also a member of the Klan, penned a detailed account of Forrest, but never definitively connects him with the leadership of the organization.[182]

One of Forrest's most important biographers, John Allan Wyeth, authored a 600-page book covering every detail of its subject's life, including the KKK period. But again, no mention of Forrest being either the Grand Wizard, a Grand Dragon (a state leader), or even a member.[183] Another significant Forrest biographer, Captain J. Harvey Mathes, devotes several pages to the KKK in his work *General Forrest* without directly connecting Ol' Bedford to the Klan.[184]

THE REAL GRAND WIZARD

Who then was the head of the original KKK? All we know is that it was not Forrest. What little circumstantial evidence exists indicates that my cousin George Washington Gordon was Grand Wizard between 1865 and 1869,[185] and, in fact, Gordon's wife, Ora Susan Paine, later testified to this.[186]

At most Forrest may have been some kind of advisor or recruiter, but even this is not known for sure.[187] Not even the all-powerful Reconstruction leaders in Washington, D.C., with their secret police force and strong-arm detectives, could find any evidence that Forrest was the organization's leader.[188]

In a book on the Reconstruction KKK written in 1905—exactly 40 years after the group's formation—Forrest is publicly called the "Grand Wizard of the Ku Klux Klan." There is no hard evidence for this assertion, however. Not only have others been named, George W. Gordon's wife, Ora S. Paine, later testified that her husband was Grand Wizard. Forrest himself denied even being a member and his biographers never mention any link between the General and the KKK. As the Reconstruction Klan never wrote anything down and old memories are untrustworthy, it is time to take Forrest and Mrs. Gordon at their word.

CLAIMS THAT FORREST WAS GRAND WIZARD

How then do we deal with the assertions of some of the original KKK members, including several cofounders, that Forrest was the Grand Wizard?

It is true that later on Forrest came to be regarded by many in the South as having once been the organization's leader. Indeed, some of the Klan's creators stated as much in their memoirs. However, since there was a death penalty for revealing such information,[189] and since other KKK members contradicted this by stating that Forrest was *not* the Grand Wizard, these assertions are automatically suspect, leaving us with several possibilities:

1) These claims were the products of *faulty memories* two or three generations after the fact (in some cases over 50 years later).[190]
2) These claims were *anecdotal* (which is subjective and biased, and therefore both unreliable and unverifiable).
3) These claims were the product of *confusion*, for other individuals have also been named the first Grand Wizard (see 5).
4) These claims were *purposeful errors* (disinformation), for attaching Forrest's prestigious name and honorable reputation to the order imbued it with a cachet of Southern power, grandeur, mysticism, and *gravitas* that it might not have had otherwise.
5) These claims were invented in order to *cover up* and *protect* the identity of the *real* Grand Wizard, who, as mentioned, was almost certainly George Washington Gordon—the same individual who it is said introduced Forrest to the Klan to begin with.

After decades of research into this "problem" I am convinced that Forrest was not the Grand Wizard of the Reconstruction KKK, though I believe he played some type of crucial role in the organization and was intimately affiliated with it on one or more levels. He did admit to supporting it after all, and never tried to hide this fact.

However, even if Forrest had been a KKK member, the Grand Dragon of Tennessee, or even the Grand Wizard of the entire order, it would not taint his reputation in my eyes or in the eyes of the rest of the traditional South. For the real Reconstruction KKK was *not* an evil, violent, or racist group, as foes of the South maintain. It was quite the opposite: it was a noble and desperately needed second manifestation of the Confederate army, defending the Constitution and the Southland from the ravages of an "implacable Northern foe."

Indeed, its six "founding fathers" were known to be "gentlemen of education and refined tastes . . . [individuals who] could not have conceived the organization of an order that had for its objects low purposes or brutal usages"[191]—such as murderousness, crime, and racial intolerance. If, in fact, it *did* possess these "objects," thousands of Northerners (including some of Lincoln's own soldiers) would not have supported the Reconstruction KKK.[192] More to the point, thousands of Southern blacks would not have assisted it, championed it,[193] joined it, or formed their own KKK den in Nashville.[194] So ends another Yankee fairy tale.

This illustration of two Mississippi Klansmen dates from the period of the Reconstruction KKK. These were not outlaws and murderers, as the North would have us believe. They were ordinary Southern family men who used the "fear factor" to maintain law and order across the former Confederacy.

FORREST IS INTERROGATED BY THE U.S. GOVERNMENT

There is more evidence that Forrest was not the Grand Wizard, this coming from the General himself.

On June 27, 1871, he was put on the witness stand before a highly prejudicial, South-loathing, U.S. governmental investigative committee on Klan activities. Forrest not only denied being the leader of the KKK, but he also disclaimed even being a member (though he did state that he was "in sympathy" with the Klan and that he had been a member of the Pale Faces, a Mason-like organization). "The KKK was nothing more than a defensive body," he rightly asserted, "organized to counter the nefarious work of the North's Freedmen's Bureau, Union League, and various Loyal Leagues," all anti-South organizations.[195]

After a severe grilling the committee sided with Forrest, finding him innocent of all charges in association with the organization,[196] and concluding that he was not and had never been either the founder of or the first leader of the Reconstruction KKK.[197] According to the *Report of the House Congressional Committee*, which interviewed Forrest and other former Confederates in 1871 and 1872:

> *The statements of these [former Confederate] gentlemen are so full and explicit that comment would only weaken their force. The evidence taken before the committee fully sustains them as to the other States relative to which evidence was heard, and it is only necessary to turn to the records and official documents of the State of Tennessee to show that all General Forrest said about the alarm which prevailed in Tennessee during the administration of Governor [William G.] Brownlow was strictly true.* No State was ever reduced to such humiliation and degradation as that unhappy commonwealth during the years Brownlow ruled over her. Her constitution was imposed upon her by a fraction of her people and the people of other States; her legislature, under the dictation of her governor, as early as 1865 began a series of acts of outlawry and oppression which drove her people almost to desperation; whatever was necessary to maintain in power the [Northern] men who had seized the reins of government was ordered and executed with a high hand, and, when necessary, at the point of the bayonet.
>
> *An act restricting suffrage was passed, which disfranchised three-fourths of the native population of Middle and West Tennessee; commissioners of registration were appointed and removed at the caprice of the governor; votes of counties by the dozen were rejected when they did not vote as ordered; acts ratifying the illegal edicts of the governor were passed by an obsequious legislature; the men who decided who should and who should not vote, who controlled the registration and elections, were the tools of the governor, when he was himself a candidate.*
>
> *The sedition law was revived, freedom of speech and of the press was overthrown, and a militia force was organized, which was responsible to the governor alone, composed principally of ignorant and debased men, under the lead of the most unscrupulous [Yankee] partisans, of course.* The [carpetbag-scallywag] rulers and their adherents were loud in their professions of loyalty, which simply meant there, as everywhere else, *subserviency to the dominant party.* Everybody was loyal who voted for and maintained Brownlow and his friends, and everybody was disloyal who dared to oppose them.[198]

Under the North's four unconstitutional and vindictive Reconstruction Acts, beautiful sprawling plantations, like this one in Marengo County, Alabama, were illegally seized by the U.S. government, their owners evicted, arrested, or even murdered, and the land parceled up and given to former slaves and wealthy carpetbaggers. No rational person can ever wonder why the Reconstruction KKK arose or why men like Forrest supported it.

SOME U.S. OFFICIALS UNDERSTOOD THE RISE OF THE KKK

In the end the U.S. government actually attained at least some understanding of why the South created the KKK to begin with, correctly saying that "misgovernment and criminal exploiting of the country by the reconstruction leaders had provoked natural resistance."[199] Even many stalwart pro-North Yankees later recognized this fact. One of them was Daniel H. Chamberlain of Massachusetts, who served as governor of South Carolina during Reconstruction. Of the Southern white man in the 1870s he said:

> *I consider him a distinct and really noble growth of our American soil.* For if fortitude under good and under evil fortune, if endurance without complaint of what comes in the tide of human affairs, if a grim clinging to ideals once charming, if vigor and resiliency of character and spirit under defeat and poverty and distress, if a steady love of learning and letters when libraries were lost in flames and the wreckage of war, if self-restraint when the long-delayed relief at last came—if, I say, all these qualities are parts of real heroism, if these qualities can vivify and ennoble a man or a people, then *our own South may lay claim to an honored place among the differing types of our great common race.*[200]

Yankee journalist Winfield Jones noted that:

> Impartial historians are now agreed that it was a mistake on the part of Congress to attempt to coerce the South, and it was also impolitic for any power to attempt to cause the Anglo-Saxon race in the South to become submerged under a black political wave. The real roots of the Ku Klux Klan can be traced back to those qualities of the Anglo-Saxon race, *existing both in the North and the South*, which forbade amalgamation of the white blood with an inferior race, and the possession of a spirit which was determined to be dominant in government at all hazards. *Had conditions been reversed the Northern people undoubtedly would have acted exactly as did the Southerners.*[201]

Jones' last sentence is absolutely true, as any historian who is familiar with the real Old North will tell you.[202]

To reemphasize: in its 1872 minority report, the U.S. government commission that investigated Forrest and the KKK stated

> that misgovernment and exploitation of the South by Reconstruction officials had provoked the natural resentment and resistance of the people of that section.[203]

Thus, as Colonel Jones continues, in one sense the U.S. government came to excuse and even justify the rise and growth of the Reconstruction KKK, for it was at this time that

> the carpetbagger and the negro legislature were officially condemned by a congressional committee . . .[204]

FORREST POST KKK

As for Forrest, after 1869, having shut down the KKK and thoroughly repudiated racial prejudice, he became an ardent civil rights advocate, pushing for equal rights for blacks,[205] topics which I address in my book *Nathan Bedford Forrest and African-Americans: Yankee Myth, Confederate Fact*.

Though this old illustration of Lincoln (on the right) is from Thomas Dixon Jr.'s 1905 book *The Clansman*, a novel about Reconstruction and the original KKK, its caption, though paraphrased, is certainly not fiction. The ailing man on the left is the "Honorable Austin Stoneman," an obvious caricature of Thaddeus Stevens, one of the South's most tyrannical foes and arguably the most radical, fanatical, and contemptuous New England Liberal to have ever walked the halls of Congress. Of this venomous character Dixon says: "The word conservatism was to him as a red rag to a bull." How true this was of Stevens! In the picture shown here Dixon has Stoneman saying angrily: "The South is conquered soil. I mean to blot it from the map," which is nearly identical with many of Stevens' real life comments. However, contrary to popular opinion—one still held by many even here in the traditional South—Lincoln was actually of the same mind, though his sycophants and biographers have long tried to hide the fact. As we have seen, in 1862 Lincoln told T. J. Barnett, an official at the Interior Department, that the real purpose of the Civil War was "subjugation," and that "the South is to be destroyed and replaced with new propositions and ideas."

5

A Summary of Forrest & the Ku Klux Klan

THE TRUTH HAS BEEN ESTABLISHED ONCE & FOR ALL

WHEN THE MYTH AND DROSS and false anti-South propaganda are cleared away, only the truth remains. When it comes to Forrest and the KKK, that truth is a bitter pill indeed for those who detest the traditional, conservative, Christian South.

But the truth will not go away just because Liberals and uneducated Conservatives wish it would, nor will it disappear by rewriting history, or by spreading insidious rumors, malicious slander, and overtly manufactured disinformation—just a few of the methods the Left uses in its ongoing war to erode and Northernize the South.

A REVIEW OF THE FACTS

Let us summarize the documented facts about Forrest and the Ku Klux Klan, both the Old and the New:

☛ Forrest did not form the Reconstruction KKK. It was founded by six men in Pulaski, Tennessee, in December 1865. Forrest was living and working in Memphis at the time. The founders' names are well-known: Captain John C. Lester, Captain John B. Kennedy, Captain James R. Crowe, Richard R. Reed, Frank O. McCord, and J. Calvin Jones.

☛ Forrest was not even aware of the KKK until late 1866 or early 1867, one to two years after its formation.

☞ While Forrest was certainly an ardent supporter of the KKK, there is no hard evidence that he was the Grand Wizard, or even a member.

☞ It is most probable that George Washington Gordon was Grand Wizard during the short life of the Reconstruction KKK.

Before the reputation of the Reconstruction Ku Klux Klan was tarnished by the lies of South-hating Liberals, Yankees, scallywags and other ne'er-do-wells, the organization was held in high esteem throughout Dixie. Here, for instance, Mrs. John B. Kennedy (left), widow of one of the founders of the Reconstruction KKK, and Mrs. Grace Meredith Newbill (right), unveil a plaque at a May 1, 1917, gathering in honor of the birthplace of the Reconstruction Klan at Pulaski, Tennessee. "The tablet was placed on the outer wall of the law office once occupied by Judge Thomas M. Jones, a former Confederate Congressman, and bears the following description: Ku Klux Klan, organized in this law office... December 24, 1865, [by] Calvin E. Jones, Frank O. McCord, Richard R. Reed, John B. Kennedy, John C. Lester, James R. Crowe." The event was attended by some 1,000 people, including high school children (who sang), a college group, the Pulaski Quintet, and members of the United Daughters of the Confederacy and United Confederate Veterans.

☛ The rumors that Forrest was the founder and Grand Wizard of the Reconstruction KKK were started by anti-South advocates shortly after the War in order to humiliate Forrest, his family, and his soldiers. As the order did not keep written records, no one can prove that either of these legends have any truth to them. And in fact, numerous people, including authentic KKK members, testified that they were patently false. Furthermore, as we have seen, unlike the Liberal North the Conservative South did not view the KKK as a "pernicious order made up of ruthless ruffians and racists," and so it would not have hurt Forrest's reputation to have been associated with it. In fact, it would have benefitted him in Dixie—which is precisely what happened.

The home of Thomas Martin, Pulaski, Tennessee, "where the organization of the [Reconstruction] Ku Klux Klan was perfected, and some of the first meetings were held. The window bearing the cross mark [lower left] was the room where the Ku Klux assembled."

☛ Claims by a few KKK members and founders that Forrest was the group's Grand Wizard do not stand up to close objective scrutiny. And, in fact, such claims are negated by other Klansmen who said that he was not, as well as by testimony that George Washington Gordon (and others) served as the group's first and only Grand Wizard. Not even the U.S. government could find any evidence that Forrest was the leader of the Reconstruction KKK. In the end, there is simply no hard proof for this assertion.

☞ Naturally, the trouble-making uninformed Yankee propagandists who started the rumors about Forrest and the Reconstruction KKK were the same ones who started the rumor that the order was a racist group. This proves that such gossip was both politically motivated and false.

☞ While a small minority of white KKK members were indeed racists, as was proven by Forrest's "General Order Number One," the Reconstruction KKK itself was not a racist organization. It was a relief-and-aid society, set up to assist Southern refugees, war widows, orphans, and Confederate veterans, whatever their skin color. This helps explain why many blacks aided, and were even tortured and died for, the Reconstruction KKK in fighting carpetbaggers and scallywags,[206] and it is why the order had thousands of black members and even an all-black Ku Klux Klan at Nashville.

If the Reconstruction KKK had been a "racist and monstrous institution," as Liberals claim, we can be sure that good Christian men like Reverend W. W. Landrum, D. D., pastor of the First Baptist Church of Atlanta, Georgia, would not have been members.

☞ During the Reconstruction KKK years Forrest threatened to shoot any whites who harassed blacks. This warning included both white Northerners and white Southerners.[207]

☞ In early 1869, when Forrest felt the organization had fulfilled its stated purpose (to aid and protect the South and her citizens), he ordered it to be closed down. Then, as S. E. F. Rose put it, having accomplished its great mission "in relieving the South from the galling yoke of Carpet-Bag rule . . . this strange and mysterious order passed out of existence forever."[208] Thus the Reconstruction KKK, which was only meant to be temporary, lasted just a little over three years.

☞ Forrest, or perhaps a leader within the KKK, had several Klan members tried and executed for ignoring Forrest's order to dissolve the group.

☛ In 1871 Forrest was questioned before a U.S. government committee investigating the Reconstruction KKK, where he was found innocent of any misconduct associated with the organization. This fact alone should end any and all disputes concerning Forrest and his relationship with the Klan.

☛ The modern nationwide KKK that was founded in 1915 by William J. Simmons has no relation whatsoever to the Reconstruction KKK of the 1860s, despite the former's claim that it is "the genuine and original Klan." Indeed, they are so completely dissimilar in every way that if the modern KKK had not borrowed the name and regalia of the Reconstruction KKK, no informed individual today would make any connection between the two. Why? Because they are completely "different in conception, organization and purpose."[209] For example, in 1915 the New KKK banned Jews, Catholics, and foreigners. The original Reconstruction KKK, however, did not exclude anyone, and, in fact, according to the testimony of former constituents, it included Jewish, Catholic, and foreign members. Another one of the many differences was that the Reconstruction KKK did not solicit members, while the New KKK did.[210]

The real banner of the Reconstruction KKK, 1865-1869, was not the Confederate Battle Flag, thus it should not be associated with either the Old KKK (1865-1869) or the New KKK (post 1915). The actual 1867 emblem of the Reconstruction KKK is shown here. Known as the "Grand Ensign," the 3' by 5' triangular pennant has a red scalloped border surrounding a yellow field with a black flying dragon in the center. Above the "Dracovolans" is the Latin motto: *Quod Semper, Quod Ubique, Quod Ab Omnibus*, meaning "What always, what everywhere, what by all, is held to be true." This motto is also used by the modern Catholic Church.

☛ The overt hypocrisy of those who denounce both Forrest and the Reconstruction KKK is evident from a single fact: not only do they never condemn modern black racist organizations, in many cases they actually condone and embrace them. The U.S. tax-payer funded Public Broadcasting System (PBS), for example, continually lambasts both the Reconstruction KKK and the New KKK, but it supported, funded, distributed, and aired a documentary put out by the Black Panthers in September 2015.

This photo from the 1920s shows a meeting of the modern or New KKK on Stone Mountain, Georgia, "where the New Klan was organized." There are so many differences between the Reconstruction Klan and the modern one that—outside the garb and name—the latter would be completely unrecognizable to Forrest.

☛ Even if Forrest had been a KKK member, the Grand Dragon of Tennessee, or even the Grand Wizard of the entire organization, it would not diminish his reputation in the traditional South. This is because the Reconstruction Klan, being merely a *temporary* social aid and protection society, was not something that any educated person would be ashamed of. To the contrary, millions of knowledgeable Southerners (and many non-Southerners) continue to celebrate the original Reconstruction KKK as a venerable and honorable organization that helped "save the South" during the outrages and crimes of the North's "Second Civil War" on Dixie.

☛ Whatever Forrest's exact relationship with the Reconstruction KKK was, the order itself was an understandable and entirely justifiable expression of Southern pride, esteem, and survival considering the dreadful circumstances imposed on it by the vindictive Liberal North during the postwar era. In 1921 Winfield Jones—as we have seen, a Copperhead—wrote that the

> Ku Klux Klan was only a manifestation of the spirit of opposition to reconstruction measures taken by the North, and the masked rider in his white robe was a symbol of the spirit of the South in revolt against carpetbag government and negro misrule. These are facts that cannot be explained away, and today our Northern historians, no matter how unpalatable the facts, recognize that conditions existing in the South in reconstruction times were intolerable. . . . As the South had been defeated on the battlefields and was absolutely bankrupt after Appomattox, the Southern people were not in a position to start another armed rebellion. But the organization of *the Ku Klux Klan undoubtedly was a form of rebellion against the tyranny of reconstruction policies.*
>
> The American Colonies revolted from Great Britain in 1776, under provocations that were not nearly as irksome and irritating as the conditions which were imposed on the South during reconstruction.[211]

SALUTING FORREST & A RIGHTEOUS ORGANIZATION

Dixie rests easy in these historical facts just as they stand, and will never cease honoring our great Confederate chieftain, General Nathan Bedford Forrest. We will also continue to memorialize those who served in the Reconstruction KKK in order to save the Southern people from the vitriolic attempts of the Lincoln and Grant administrations to reconstruct them in the North's image after the War.

Forrest would certainly have concurred with one of the KKK's founders, John B. Kennedy, who in 1914 wrote:

A "brother" from the original Reconstruction KKK "on duty."

The Ku Klux Klans were composed of the very best citizens of our country; their mission was to protect the weak and oppressed during the dark days of Reconstruction. To protect the women of the South, who were the loveliest, most noble and best women in the world. The survivors are old men now, old with their memories of other days long past, to cheer them during life's twilight. They are proud they were Ku Klux, and could give aid to these dear Southern women again during the Reconstruction period, for it was a dark and distressing era in our beloved Southland. We did nothing to make us ashamed; our acts were always for the good of our country and those we loved. After the lapse of all these years, the survivors of the Ku Klux Klan are gratified to hear the verdict of many who say to us, "Well done; you undoubtedly saved the beautiful Southland during the Reconstruction era."[212]

Thus terminates our history of General Forrest and "that much misunderstood and shamefully slandered organization of the Reconstruction period,"[213] the original KKK. Despite the disinformation Liberals have concocted concerning the order—another Leftist attempt to divide the country racially—today all educated traditional Southerners continue to think of it as a "remarkable organization whose services were of untold value to the South during a dark period of her history."[214]

This was in great part because of its association with one of the noblest, bravest, brightest, most famous, romantic, and faithful patriots ever to grace the pages of American history: Nathan Bedford Forrest. May his name and memory live forever in the hearts of all true Americans and lovers of liberty, whatever their race, creed, nationality, or skin color.

Forrest in 1875. After 1861 the General did not experience a free South again until the last year of his life in 1877, the same year Reconstruction ended. He served the South proudly in two wars on her people, traditions, and territory.

The End

Appendices

Additional material throwing further light on
the reasons for the emergence of and Forrest's
subsequent support of the Reconstruction KKK

118   NATHAN BEDFORD FORREST & THE KU KLUX KLAN

A midnight meeting of the Reconstruction KKK in Tennessee, 1867. South-haters will tell you that the black man lying bound and blindfolded on the ground is a victim of the Klan's "violent racist policies," and that he is about to be hanged "because he is black." Nothing could be further from the truth. This particular African-American is a scallywag who has been interfering with Southern politics and physically threatening conservative white and black Southerners. He will be "scared to death," then run out of town, hopefully never to be seen in the South again. In fact, some of the individuals under the hooded robes in the background are black men. Yankee myths die hard—but die they must. Forrest himself said of the Reconstruction Ku Klux Klan: "We are not the enemy of the blacks.... We reiterate that we are for peace and law and order. No man, white or black, shall be molested for his political sentiments. This Klan is not a political party; it is not a military party; it is a protective organization, and will never use violence except in resisting violence."

Appendix A

The First of Two Anti-South Freedmen's Bureau Acts Issued by the Liberal North Even Before the End of the War

- FIRST FREEDMEN'S BUREAU ACT -

MARCH 3, 1865

Be it enacted: That there is hereby established in the War Department, to continue *during the present war of rebellion*, and for one year thereafter, a Bureau of Refugees, Freedmen, and Abandoned Lands, to which shall be committed, as hereinafter provided, the supervision and management of all abandoned lands [there was no such thing as "abandoned lands" or "abandoned plantations" in the South; the owners were either driven off or killed], and the control of all subjects relating to refugees and freedmen from rebel States, or from any district of country within the territory embraced in the operations of the army, under such rules and regulations as may be prescribed by the head of the bureau and approved by the President. The said bureau shall be under the management and control of a commissioner, to be appointed by the President, by and with the advice and consent of the Senate, whose compensation shall be three thousand dollars per annum, and such number of clerks as may be assigned to him by the Secretary of War, not exceeding one chief clerk, two of the fourth class, two of the third class, and five of the first class. And the commissioner, and all persons appointed under this act, shall, before entering upon their duties, take the ["iron clad" test oath] and the commissioner and chief clerk shall, before entering upon their duties, give bonds to the Treasurer of the United States, the former in the sum of fifty thousand dollars, and the latter in the sum of ten thousand dollars, conditioned for the faithful discharge of their duties.

Sec. 2. The Secretary of War may direct such issues or provisions, clothing and fuel as he may deem needful for the immediate and temporary shelter and supply of destitute and suffering refugees and freedmen, and their wives and children.

Sec. 3. The President may, by and with the advice and consent of the Senate, *appoint an assistant commissioner for each of the States declared to be in insurrection*, not exceeding ten in number, who shall, under the direction of the commissioner, aid in the execution of the provisions of this act; and he shall give a bond to the Treasurer of the United States, in the sum of twenty thousand dollars. Each of said [assistant] commissioners shall receive an annual salary of two thousand five hundred dollars in full compensation for all his services; and any military officer may be detailed and assigned to duty under this act without increase of pay or allowances. The commissioner shall, before the commencement of each regular session of Congress, make full report of his proceedings, with exhibits of the state of his accounts, to the President, who shall communicate the same to Congress, and shall also make special reports whenever required to do so by the President or either house of Congress; and the assistant commissioners shall make quarterly reports of their proceedings to the commissioner, and also such other special reports as from time to time may be required.

Sec. 4. *The commissioner, under the direction of the President, shall have authority to set apart, for the use of loyal refugees and freedmen, such tracts of lands within the insurrectionary States as shall have been abandoned, or to which the United States shall have acquired title by confiscation or sale, or otherwise; and to every male citizen, whether refugee or freedman, as aforesaid, there shall be assigned not more than forty acres of such land*, and the person to whom it was so assigned shall be protected in the use and enjoyment of the land for the term of three years at an annual rent not exceeding six *per centum* upon the value of such land as it was appraised by the State authorities in the year eighteen hundred and sixty for the purpose of taxation; and in case no such appraisal can be found, then the rental shall be based upon the estimated value of the land in said year, to be ascertained in such manner as the commissioner may by regulation prescribe. At the end of said term, or at any time during said term, *the occupants of any parcels so assigned may purchase the land and receive such title thereto as the United States can convey*, upon paying therefor the value of the land as ascertained and fixed for the purpose of determining the annual rent aforesaid.[215]

Appendix B

The Second of Two Anti-South Freedmen's Bureau Acts Issued by the Liberal North

- SECOND FREEDMEN'S BUREAU ACT -

JULY 16, 1866

Be it enacted: That the act to establish a Bureau for the relief of Freedmen and Refugees, approved March third, eighteen hundred sixty-five, shall continue in force for the term of two years from and after the passage of this act.

Sec. 2. The supervision and care of said bureau shall extend to all *loyal refugees and freedmen*, so far as the same may be necessary to enable them as speedily as practicable to become self-supporting citizens of the United States, and to aid them in making the freedom conferred by the proclamation of the Commander-in-Chief, by emancipation under the laws of the States, and by constitutional amendment, available to them and beneficial to the Republic.

Sec. 3. The President shall, by and with the consent of the Senate, appoint two assistant commissioners, in addition to those authorized by the act to which this is an amendment, who shall give like bonds and receive the same annual salaries provided in said act; and each of the assistant commissioners of the bureau shall have charge of the district containing such refugees or freedmen, to be assigned him by the Commissioner, with the approval of the President. And the Commissioner shall, under the direction of the President, and so far as the same shall be, in his judgment, necessary for the efficient and economical administration of the affairs of the bureau, appoint such agents, clerks and assistants as may be required for the proper conduct of the bureau. Military officers or enlisted men may be detailed for service and assigned to duty under this act; and the President may, if in his judgment safe and judicious so to do, detail from the Army all the officers and agents of the bureau; but no officer so assigned shall have increase of pay or allowances. Each agent or clerk, not heretofore authorized by law, not being a military officer, shall have an annual salary of not less than $500, nor more than $1,200, according to the service required of him. And it shall be the duty of the Commissioner, when it can be done consistently with the public interest, to appoint, as assistant commissioners, agents, and clerks, such *men as have proved their loyalty by faithful service in the armies of the Union during the rebellion.* And all persons appointed to service under this act and the act to which this is an amendment, shall be so far deemed in the military service of the United States as to be under the military jurisdiction and entitled to the military protection of the Government while in the discharge of the duties of their office.

Sec. 4. The officers of the Veteran Reserve Corps or of the volunteer service, now on duty in the Freedmen's Bureau as assistant commissioners, agents, medical officers, or in other capacities, whose regiments or corps have been or may hereafter be mustered out of service, may be retained upon such duty as officers of said bureau, with the same compensation as is now provided by law for their respective grades; and the Secretary of War shall have power to fill vacancies until other officers can be detailed in their places without detriment to the public service.

Sec. 5. The second section of the act to which this is an amendment shall be deemed to authorize the Secretary of War to issue such medical stores or other supplies and transportation and afford such medical or other aid as may be needful for the purposes named in said section: Provided, that no person shall be deemed "destitute," "suffering," or "dependent upon the Government for support," within the meaning of this act, who is able to find employment, and could, by proper industry and exertion, avoid such destitution, suffering, or dependency.

Sec. 6. Whereas, by the provisions of [an act of February 6, 1863, vetoed by President Andrew Johnson] *certain lands in the parishes of St. Helena and St. Luke, South Carolina, were bid in by the United States at public tax sales,* and by limitation of said act the time of redemption of said lands has expired; and whereas, in accordance with instructions issued by President Lincoln on [September 16, 1863] to the United States direct tax commissioners of South Carolina, *certain lands bid in by the United States in the parish of St. Helena, in said State, were in part sold by the said tax commissioners to "heads of families of the African race," in parcels of not more than twenty acres to each purchaser; and whereas, under the said instructions, the said tax commissioners did also set apart as "school farms" certain parcels of land in said parish, numbered on their plats from one to thirty-three inclusive, making an aggregate of six thousand acres, more or less: Therefore, be it further enacted,* That the sales made to "heads of families of the African race," under the instructions of President Lincoln to the United States direct tax commissioners for South Carolina, are hereby confirmed and established; and all leases which have been made to such "heads of families" by said direct tax commissioners, shall be changed into certificates of sale in all cases wherein the lease provides for such substitution; and all the lands now remaining unsold, which come within the same designation, being eight thousand acres, more or less, shall be disposed of according to said instructions.

Reconstruction was merely a 12 year extension of the Civil War and the Ku Klux Klan of that period was merely a civilian manifestation of the Confederate army. Those who say anything different are either lying or are ignorant of the facts.

Sec. 7. All other lands bid in by the United States at tax sales, being thirty-eight thousand acres, more or less, and now in the hands of the said tax commissioners as the property of the United States, in the parishes of St. Helena and St. Luke, excepting the "school farms," as specified in the preceding section, and so much as may be necessary for military and naval purposes at Hilton Head, Bay Point, and Land's End, and excepting also the city of Port Royal on St. Helena island, and the town of Beaufort, shall be disposed of in parcels of twenty acres, at one dollar and fifty cents per acre, to such persons, and to such only, as have acquired and are now occupying lands under and agreeably to the provisions of General Sherman's special field order, dated at Savannah, Georgia, [January 16, 1865] and the remaining lands, if any, shall be disposed of in like manner to such persons as had acquired lands agreeably to the said order of General Sherman but who have been dispossessed by the restoration of the same to former owners: Provided, That the lands sold in compliance with the provisions of this and the preceding section shall not be alienated by their purchasers within six years from and after the passage of this act.

Sec. 8. The "school farms" shall be sold, and the proceeds of said sales shall be invested in United States bonds, the interest of which shall be appropriated, under the direction of the Commissioner, to the support of schools, without distinction of color or race, on the islands in the parishes of St. Helena and St. Luke.

Sec. 9. The assistant commissioners for South Carolina and Georgia are hereby authorized to examine all claims to lands in their respective States which are claimed under the provisions of General Sherman's special field order, and to give each person having a valid claim a warrant upon the direct tax commissioners for South Carolina for twenty acres of land; and the said direct tax commissioners shall issue to every person, or to his or her heirs, but in no case to any assigns, presenting such warrant, a lease of twenty acres of land, as provided for in section seven, for the term of six years; but at any time thereafter, upon the payment of a sum not exceeding one dollar and fifty cents per acre, the person holding such lease shall be entitled to a certificate of sale of said tract of twenty acres from the direct tax commissioner or such officer as may be authorized to issue the same; but no warrant shall be held valid longer than two years after the issue of the same.

Sec. 10. The tax commissioners for South Carolina are hereby authorized and required, at the earliest day practicable, to survey the lands designated in section seven into lots of twenty acres each, with proper metes and bounds distinctly marked, so that the several tracts shall be convenient in form, and as near as practicable have an average of fertility and woodland.

Sec. 11. *Restoration of lands occupied by freedmen under General Sherman's field order* dated at Savannah, Georgia, [January 16, 1865] shall not be made until after the crops of the present year shall have been gathered by the occupants of said lands, nor until a fair compensation shall have been made to them by the former owners of such lands, or their legal representatives, for all improvements or betterments erected or constructed thereon, and after due notice of the same being done shall have been given by the assistant commissioner.

Sec. 12. *The Commissioner shall have power to seize, hold, use, lease, or sell all buildings, and tenements, and any lands appertaining to the same, or otherwise, formerly held under color of title by the late so-called Confederate States* [the writer is obviously ignorant of the fact that the U.S.A. itself was once called the "Confederate States"],[216] *and not heretofore disposed of by the United States, and any buildings or lands held in trust for the same by any person or persons, and to use the same or appropriate the proceeds derived therefrom to the education of the freed people; and whenever the bureau shall cease to exist, such of said so-called Confederate States as shall have made provision for the education of their citizens without distinction of color shall receive the sum remaining unexpended of such sales or rentals, which shall be distributed among said States for educational purposes in proportion to their population.*

Sec. 13. *The Commissioner of this bureau shall at all times co-operate with private benevolent associations of citizens in aid of freedmen, and with agents and teachers, duly accredited and appointed by them, and shall hire or provide by lease, buildings for purposes of education whenever such associations shall, without cost to the Government, provide suitable teachers and means of instruction; and he shall furnish such protection as may be required for the safe conduct of such schools.*

Sec. 14. *In every State or district when the ordinary course of judicial proceedings has been interrupted by* the rebellion, *and until the same shall be fully restored, and in every State or district whose constitutional relations to the Government have been practically discontinued by the rebellion, and until such State shall have been restored in such relations, and shall be duly represented in the Congress of the United States, the right to make and enforce contracts, to sue, be parties, and give evidence, to inherit, purchase, lease, sell, hold, and convey real and personal property, and to have full and equal benefit of all laws and proceedings concerning personal liberty, personal security, and the acquisition, enjoyment, and disposition of estate, real and personal, including the constitutional right to bear arms, shall be secured to and enjoyed by all the citizens of such State or district without respect to race or color, or previous condition of slavery. And whenever in either of said States or districts the ordinary course of judicial proceedings has been* interrupted by the rebellion, and until the same shall be fully restored, and until such State shall have been restored to its constitutional relations to the Government, and shall be duly represented in the Congress of the United States, the President shall, through the Commissioner and the officers of the bureau, and under such rules and regulations as the President, through the Secretary of War, shall prescribe, extend military protection and have military jurisdiction over all cases and questions concerning the free enjoyment of such immunities and rights; and no penalty or punishment for any violation of law shall be imposed or permitted because of race or color, or previous condition of slavery, other or greater than the penalty or punishment to which the white persons may be liable by law for the like offense. But the jurisdiction conferred by this section upon the officers of the bureau shall not exist in any State where the ordinary course of judicial proceedings has not been interrupted by *the rebellion*, and shall cease in every State when the courts of the State and the United States are not disturbed in the peaceable course of justice, and after such State shall be fully restored in its constitutional relations to the Government, and shall be duly represented in the Congress of the United States.

Sec. 15. That all officers, agents, and employees of this bureau, before entering upon the duties of their office, shall take the ["iron clad" test oath].[217]

My cousin Ellen Bourne Tynes, the second wife of Captain John W. Morton of Nashville, Tennessee, Forrest's chief of artillery during the War and his friend afterward. Like millions of other Southerners of all races, both Mr. and Mrs. Morton supported the Reconstruction KKK and were intimately associated with it. Despite this familiarity, in his memoirs John never personally connects Forrest with the position of Grand Wizard.

Appendix C

The First of Four Anti-South Reconstruction Acts Issued by the Liberal North

- THE MILITARY GOVERNMENT BILL -
AN ACT FOR THE MORE EFFICIENT
GOVERNMENT OF THE REBEL STATES

MARCH 2, 1867

Whereas, No legal State government, or adequate protection for life, or property, now exists in the rebel States of Virginia, North Carolina, South Carolina, Georgia, Alabama, Louisiana, Florida, Texas, and Arkansas; and,

Whereas, It is necessary that peace and good order should be enforced in said States until loyal and republican State governments can be established; therefore,

Be it enacted, etc., That said rebel [former Confederate] States shall be divided into military districts, and made subject to the military authority of the United States, as hereinafter prescribed; and for that purpose Virginia shall constitute the first district; North Carolina and South Carolina the second district; Georgia, Alabama, und Florida the third district; Mississippi and Arkansas the fourth district; Louisiana and Texas the fifth district.

Sec. 2. That it shall be the duty of the [U.S.] President to assign to the command of each of said districts an officer of the [U.S.] army, not below the rank of brigadier-general, and to detail a sufficient military force to enable such officer to perform his duties and enforce his authority within the district to which he is assigned.

Sec. 3. That it shall be the duty of each [U.S.] officer assigned, as aforesaid, to protect all persons in their rights of person and property; to suppress insurrection, disorder, and violence, and to punish, and cause to be punished, all disturbers of the public peace, and criminals; and to this end he may allow loyal civil tribunals to take jurisdiction of and try offenders; or, when in his judgment it may be necessary, for the trial of offenders, he shall have power to organize military commissions or tribunals for that purpose; and all interference under color of State authority with the exercise of military authority under this act shall be null and void.

Sec. 4. That all persons put under military arrest by virtue of this act shall be tried without unnecessary delay, and no cruel or unusual punishment shall be inflicted, and no sentence of any military commission or tribunal, hereby authorized, affecting the life or liberty of any person, shall be executed until it is approved by the officer in command of the district; and the laws and regulations for the government of the army shall not be affected by this act, except in so far as they may conflict with its provisions.

Colonel Leroy McAfee, a former Confederate officer and the uncle of Thomas Dixon Jr., was a typical leader of the Reconstruction Ku Klux Klan.

Sec. 5. That when the people of any one of said rebel States shall have formed a constitutional government, in conformity with the Constitution of the United States in all respects, framed by a convention of delegates elected by the persons who may vote upon the ratification or rejection thereof, as hereinafter provided; and when said constitution, so framed, shall have been ratified by a majority of the male citizens of said State, twenty-one years old and upward, of whatever race, color, or previous condition of servitude, who may have been resident in said State for one year previous to the day of voting on the question of ratifying such constitution, except such as may be disfranchised for participating in the rebellion, or for felony at common law; and when such constitution shall provide that the elective franchise shall be enjoyed by all such persons that have the qualifications herein stated, and shall have been submitted to Congress for examination, and Congress shall have approved the same; and when said State, by a vote of its legislature elected under said constitution, shall have adopted the amendment to the Constitution of the United States, proposed by the Thirty-ninth Congress, and known as article fourteen, and when said article shall become a part of the Constitution of the United States, such State shall be declared entitled to representation in Congress, and senators and representatives shall be admitted thereupon, on their taking the oath prescribed by the law; and then and thereafter the preceding sections of this bill shall be inoperative in said State.

Sec. 6, (proposed by Mr. [James R.] Doolittle,) provides that the penalty of death shall not be inflicted by the military power without the approval of the President.

Sec. 7. ([Samuel] Shellabarger's amendment.) That until the people of said rebel States shall, by law, be admitted to representation in the Congress of the United States, the civil governments that may exist therein shall be deemed provisional only, and shall be in all respects subject to the paramount authority of the United States, which may at any time abolish, modify, control, and supersede the same, and in all elections to any office under such provisional governments all persons shall be entitled to vote, and none others, who are entitled to vote under the provisions of the fifth section of this act, and no person shall be eligible to any office under such provisional governments who would be disqualified from holding office under the provisions of the third article of said Constitutional Amendment.[218]

Richmond, Virginia, in ruins, April 1865.

Confederate General Albert Pike of Boston, Massachusetts, was not only a teacher, attorney, editor, poet, and author, he was also the Father of Scottish Rite Masonry in the United States, as well as the Chief Judicial Officer of the Reconstruction Ku Klux Klan. Pike is wearing a Masonic sash with "33" on it, the number of degrees of initiation attainable within the organization. The number 33 is a doubling of the number of the Holy Trinity: God (Mind), Jesus (Body), and the Holy Ghost (Spirit). Hanging from Pike's sash is the archetypal double-headed phoenix, an ancient symbol of immortality, resurrection, and rebirth (i.e., being "born again" in new wisdom), for the phoenix in ancient Egyptian mythology arose from the ashes at Heliopolis after three days. In the early Christian Church the phoenix was absorbed as a symbol of the immortal soul and the resurrection of Jesus on the third day. These ties between Christianity, Masonry, and the Reconstruction KKK are seldom discussed, but are important to any true understanding of the original Ku Klux Klan, 1865-1869.

Appendix D

The Second of Four Anti-South Reconstruction Acts Issued by the Liberal North

- SUPPLEMENT TO THE MILITARY GOVERNMENT BILL - PASSED AT THE FIRST SESSION OF THE FORTIETH CONGRESS

MARCH 23, 1867

An Act supplementary to an act entitled, "An act to provide for the more efficient government of the rebel States," passed March second, eighteen hundred and sixty-seven, and to facilitate restoration.

Be it enacted by the Senate and House of Representatives of the United States of America in Congress assembled, That before the first day of September, eighteen hundred and sixty-seven, the commanding general in each district defined by an act entitled, "An act to provide for the more efficient government of the rebel States," passed March second, eighteen hundred and sixty-seven, shall cause a registration to be made of the male citizens of the United States, twenty-one years of age and upward, resident in each county or parish in the State or States included in his district, which registration shall include only those persons who are qualified to vote for delegates by the act aforesaid, and who shall have taken and subscribed the following oath or affirmation: "I, _____, do solemnly swear, (or affirm,) in the presence of Almighty God, that I am a citizen of the State of _____; that I have resided in said State for _____ months next preceding this day, and now reside in the county of _____, or the parish of _____, in said State, (as the case may be;) that I am twenty-one years old; that I have not been disfranchised for participation in any rebellion or civil war against the United States, nor for felony committed against the laws of any State or of the United

States; that I have never been a member of any State legislature, nor held any executive or judicial office in any State, and afterward engaged in insurrection or rebellion against the United States, or given aid or comfort to the enemies thereof; that I have never taken an oath as a member of Congress of the United States, or as an officer of the United States, or as a member of any State legislature, or as an executive or judicial officer of any State, to support the Constitution of the United States, and afterward engaged in insurrection or rebellion against the United States, or given aid or comfort to the enemies thereof; that I will faithfully support the Constitution and obey the laws of the United States, and will, to the best of my ability, encourage others so to do, so help me God;" which oath or affirmation may be administered by any registering officer.

This old illustration shows one of the results of Reconstruction: a white Southerner is on his knees polishing the boots of a former slave, as an imperious carpetbagger looks on. It was not the role reversal that white Southerners objected to during Reconstruction. It was that the Liberal North had invaded Dixie a second time in an attempt to impose its will on her at the tip of a gun barrel. Of course, disrupting Southern society by pitting the races against one another was all part of the North's plan to begin with, just another reason for the emergence of the Reconstruction KKK.

Sec. 2. And be it further enacted, That after the completion of the registration hereby provided for in any State, at such time and places therein as the commanding general shall appoint and direct, of which at least thirty days' public notice shall be given, an election shall be held of delegates to a convention for the purpose of establishing a constitution and civil government for such State loyal to the Union, said convention in each State, except Virginia, to consist of the same number of members as the most numerous branch of the State legislature of such State in the year eighteen hundred and sixty, to be apportioned among the several districts, counties, or parishes of such State by the commanding general, giving to each representation in the ratio of voters registered as aforesaid as nearly as may be. The convention in Virginia shall consist of the same number of members as represented the territory now constituting Virginia in the most numerous branch of the legislature of said State in the year eighteen hundred and sixty, to be apportioned as aforesaid.

Sec. 3. And be it further enacted, That at said election the registered voters of each State shall vote for or against a convention to form a constitution therefor under this act. Those voting in favor of such a convention shall have written or printed on the ballots by which they vote for delegates, as aforesaid, the words, "For a convention;" and those voting against such a convention shall have written or printed on such ballots the words, "Against a convention." The persons appointed to superintend said election, and to make return of the votes given thereat, as herein provided, shall count and make return of the votes given for and against a convention; and the commanding general to whom the same shall have been returned shall ascertain and declare the total vote in each State for and against a convention. If a majority of the votes given on that question shall be for a convention, then such convention shall be held as hereinafter provided; but if a majority of said votes shall be against a convention, then no such convention shall be held under this act: Provided, That such convention shall not be held unless a majority of all such registered voters shall have voted on the question of holding such convention.

Sec. 4. And be it further enacted, That the commanding general of each district shall appoint as many boards of registration as may be necessary, consisting of three loyal officers or persons, to make and complete the registration, superintend the election, and make return to him of the votes, list of voters, and of the persons elected as delegates, by a plurality of the votes cast at said election; and upon receiving said returns, he shall open the same, ascertain the persons elected as delegates, according to the returns of the officers who conducted said election, and make proclamation thereof; and if a majority of the votes given on that question shall be for a convention, the commanding general, within sixty days from the date of election, shall notify the delegates to assemble in convention, at a time and place to be mentioned in the notification; and said convention, when organized, shall proceed to frame a constitution and civil government according to the provisions of this act, and the act to which it is supplementary; and when the same shaft have been so framed, said constitution shall be submitted by the convention for ratification to the persons' registered under the provisions of this act, at an election to be conducted by the officers or persons appointed or to be appointed by the commanding general, as hereinbefore provided, and to be held after the expiration of thirty days from the date of notice thereof, to be given by said convention; and the returns thereof shall be made to the commanding general of the district.

Sec. 5. And be it further enacted, That if, according to said returns, the constitution shall be ratified by a majority of the votes of the registered electors qualified as herein specified, cast at said election, at least one-half of all the registered voters voting upon the question of such ratification, the president of the convention shall transmit a copy of the same, duly certified, to the President of the United States, who shall forthwith transmit the same to Congress, if then in session, and if not in session, then immediately upon its next assembling; and if it shall moreover appear to Congress that the election was one at which all the registered and qualified electors in the State had an opportunity to vote freely and without restraint, fear, or the influence of fraud, and if the Congress shall be satisfied that such constitution meets the approval of a majority of all the qualified electors in the State, and if the said constitution shall be declared by Congress to be in conformity with the provisions of the act to which this is supplementary, and the other provisions of said act shall have been complied with, and the said constitution shall be approved by Congress, the State shall be declared entitled to representation, and senators and representatives shall be admitted therefrom, as therein provided.

Sec. 6. And be it further enacted, That all elections in the States mentioned in the said "Act to provide for the more efficient government of the rebel States," shall, during the operation of said act, be by ballot; and all officers making the said registration of voters and conducting said elections shall, before entering upon the discharge of their duties, take and subscribe the oath prescribed by the act approved July second, eighteen hundred and sixty-two, entitled, "An act to prescribe an oath of office:" Provided, That if any person shall knowingly and falsely take and subscribe any oath in this act prescribed, such person so offending, and being thereof duly convicted, shall be subject to the pains, penalties, and disabilities which by law are provided for the punishment of the crime of willful and corrupt perjury.

Sec. 7. And be it further enacted, That all expenses incurred by the several commanding generals, or by virtue of any orders issued, or appointments made, by them, under or by virtue of this act, shall be paid out of any moneys in the treasury not otherwise appropriated.

Sec. 8. And be it further enacted, That the convention for each State shall prescribe the fees, salary, and compensation to be paid to all delegates and other officers and agents herein authorized or necessary to carry into effect the purposes of this act not herein otherwise provided for, and shall provide for the levy and collection of such taxes on the property in such State as may be necessary to pay the same.

Sec. 9. And be it further enacted, That the word "article" in the sixth section of the act to which this is supplementary, shall be construed to mean "section."

Schuyler Colfax, Speaker of the House of Representatives.
Benjamin F. Wade, President of the Senate pro tempore.[219]

Yankee Liberal Schuyler Colfax of New York served as America's seventeenth vice president during Reconstruction. As such, he and President Grant were responsible for much of the damage and outrages that were committed against the prostrate South during the late 1860s and early 1870s.

A typically overdone and greatly exaggerated piece of pro-North propaganda entitled "Reconstruction." In this highly symbolic 1867 lithograph, the Yankee artist shows the U.S. undergoing reconstruction after the Civil War, with the Confederate states being "reformed" and brought back into the Union once again. At the top center, Jesus—who is surrounded by everyone from Abraham Lincoln and Joan of Arc to Daniel Webster and John Milton—is saying "Do to others as you would have them do to you," while at the base of the foundation stones under the dome Confederates Robert E. Lee and Pierre G. T. Beauregard are shaking hands with Yankees Ulysses S. Grant and Benjamin F. Butler. At the bottom front center a white baby and a black baby sleep peacefully, while above them an eagle carries a banner reading: "All men are born free and equal." There are too many absurd lies, diabolical deceits, demonstrable falsehoods, and outright misrepresentations depicted to discuss here, and all of them have been covered in my other books. However, we can be sure of one thing: if the North had been as benevolent, egalitarian, charitable, and Christlike as this anti-South allegorical fantasy asserts it was, there would have been no need for a welfare, social aid, and protective society in the South, and the Reconstruction Ku Klux Klan would have never been born. The truth of the matter is that the North's behavior during Reconstruction was the opposite of how it is portrayed in this illustration. The Yankees' Freedmen's Bureau alone, for example, committed untold numbers of crimes and offences against Southern whites and blacks, none of which are ever discussed in pro-North history books—and for obvious reasons. But the facts about Reconstruction do not disappear merely because South-haters ignore or suppress them. They live on and on until they are brought back into the light. One of these unconquerable facts pertains to how the Southern people really felt about the Freedmen's Bureau. According to one honest Yankee historian, the institution "was cordially detested by the greater part of the white people of the South who saw in the bureau only a diabolical device for perpetuating the national government's control over the South and for the humiliation of the whites before their former slaves."

Appendix E

The Third of Four Anti-South Reconstruction Acts Issued by the Liberal North

SUPPLEMENT TO AN ACT ENTITLED
"AN ACT TO PROVIDE FOR THE MORE EFFICIENT
GOVERNMENT OF THE REBEL STATES"

JUNE 19, 1867

Be it enacted . . . , That it is hereby declared to have been the true intent and meaning . . . [of the acts of March 2 and March 23, 1867] . . . , that the governments then existing in the rebel States of Virginia, North Carolina, South Carolina, Georgia, Mississippi, Alabama, Louisiana, Florida, Texas, and Arkansas were not legal State governments; and that thereafter said governments, if continued, were to be continued subject in all respects to the military commanders of the respective districts, and to the paramount authority of Congress.

Sec. 2. And be it further enacted, That the commander of any district named in said act shall have power, subject to the disapproval of the General of the army of the United States, and to have effect till disapproved, whenever in the opinion of such commander the proper administration of said act shall require it, to suspend or remove from office, or from the performance of official duties and the exercise of official powers, any officer or person holding or exercising, or professing to hold or exercise, any civil or military office or duty in such district under any power, election, appointment or authority derived from, or granted by, or claimed under, any so-called State or the government thereof, or any municipal or other division thereof, and upon such suspension or removal such commander, subject to the disapproval of the General as aforesaid, shall have power to provide from time to time for the performance of the said duties of such officer or person so suspended or removed, by the detail of some competent officer or soldier of the army, or by the appointment of some other person, to perform the same, and to fill vacancies occasioned by death, resignation, or otherwise.

  Sec. 3. And be it further enacted, That the General of the army of the United States shall be invested with all the powers of suspension, removal, appointment, and detail granted in the preceding section to district commanders.

  Sec. 4. And be it further enacted, That the acts of the officers of the army already done in removing in said districts persons exercising the functions of civil officers, and appointing others in their stead, are hereby confirmed: Provided, That any person heretofore or hereafter appointed by any district commander to exercise the functions of any civil office, may be removed either by the military officer in command of the district, or by the General of the army. And it shall be the duty of such commander to remove from office as aforesaid all persons who are disloyal to the government of the United States, or who use their official influence in any manner to hinder, delay, prevent, or obstruct the due and proper administration of this act and the acts to which it is supplementary.

This Southern black family hiding in the Louisiana swamps in 1873 is not running from the Reconstruction KKK, which had been organized to help protect both whites *and* blacks from the crimes and atrocities of Federal soldiers, carpetbaggers, and scallywags. It is trying to escape the North's Union League, which, under Liberal Yankee Reconstruction policies, was bribing African-Americans to injure, even murder, their former white friends and owners—something the majority of Southern blacks were fully opposed to.

  Sec. 5. And be it further enacted, That the boards of registration provided for in the act . . . [of March 23, 1867] . . . , shall have power, and it shall be their duty before allowing the registration of any person, to ascertain, upon such facts or information as they can obtain, whether such person is entitled to be registered under said act, and the oath required by said act shall not be conclusive on such question, and no person shall be registered unless such board shall decide that he is entitled thereto; and such board shall also have power to examine, under oath, . . . any one touching the qualification of any person claiming registration; but in every case of refusal by the board to register an applicant, and in every case of striking his name from the list as hereinafter provided, the board shall make a note or memorandum, which shall be returned with the registration list to the commanding general of the district, setting forth the grounds of such refusal or such striking from the list: Provided, That no person shall be disqualified as member of any board of registration by reason of race or color.

Sec. 6. And be it further enacted, That the true intent and meaning of the oath prescribed in said supplementary act is, (among other things,) that *no person who has been a member of the legislature of any State, or who has held any executive or judicial office in any State, whether he has taken an oath to support the Constitution of the United States or not, and whether he was holding such office at the commencement of the rebellion, or had held it before, and who has afterwards engaged in insurrection or rebellion against the United States, or given aid or comfort to the enemies thereof, is entitled to be registered or to vote*; and the words "executive or judicial office in any State" in said oath mentioned shall be construed to include all civil offices created by law for the administration of any general law of a State, or for the administration of justice.

Sec. 7. And be it further enacted, That the time for completing the original registration provided for in said act may, in the discretion of the commander of any district, be extended to . . . [October 1, 1867] . . . ; and the boards of registration shall have power, and it shall be their duty, commencing fourteen days prior to any election under said act, and upon reasonable public notice of the time and place thereof, to revise, for a period of five days, the registration lists, and upon being satisfied that any person not entitled thereto has been registered, to strike the name of such person from the list, and such person shall not be allowed to vote. And such board shall also, during the same period, add to such registry the names of all persons who at that time possess the qualifications required by said act who have not been already registered; and no person shall, at any time, be entitled to be registered or to vote by reason of any executive pardon or amnesty for any act or thing which, without such pardon or amnesty, would disqualify him from registration or voting.

Sec. 8. And be it further enacted, That section four of said last-named act shall be construed to authorize the commanding general named therein, whenever he shall deem it needful, to remove any member of a board of registration and to appoint another in his stead, and to fill any vacancy in such board.

Sec. 9. And be it further enacted, That all members of said boards of registration and all persons hereafter elected or appointed to office in said military districts, under any so-called State or municipal authority, or by detail or appointment of the district commanders, shall be required to take and to subscribe the oath of office prescribed by law for officers of the United States.

Sec. 10. And be it further enacted, That no district commander or member of the board of registration, or any of the officers or appointees acting under them, shall be bound in his action by any opinion of any civil officer of the United States.

Sec. 11. And be it further enacted, That all provisions of this act and of the acts to which this is supplementary shall be construed liberally, to the end that all the intents thereof may be fully and perfectly carried out.[220]

In this illustration the people of Columbia, South Carolina, joyfully celebrate the victorious return of Wade Hampton as governor of the state in 1877. His election, along with that of the new U.S. President Rutherford B. Hayes, marked the end of Reconstruction. Confederate General Hampton, some of whose property had been destroyed by Sherman during the War, was a strong supporter of the Reconstruction KKK.

Appendix F

The Fourth of Four Anti-South Reconstruction Acts Issued by the Liberal North

AN ACT TO AMEND THE ACT OF MARCH 23, 1867 & FACILITATE THE RESTORATION OF THE LATE REBEL STATES

MARCH 11, 1868

Be it enacted . . . , That hereafter any election authorized by the act [of March 23, 1867] . . . , shall be decided by a majority of the votes actually cast; and at the election in which the question of the adoption or rejection of any constitution is submitted, any person duly registered in the State may vote in the election district where he offers to vote when he has resided therein for ten days next preceding such election, upon presentation of his certificate of registration, his affidavit, or other satisfactory evidence, under such regulations as the district commanders may prescribe.

Sec. 2. And be it further enacted, That the constitutional convention of any of the States mentioned in the acts to which this is amendatory may provide that at the time of voting upon the ratification of the constitution the registered voters may vote also for members of the House of Representatives of the United States, and for all elective officers provided for by the said constitution; and the same election officers who shall make the return of the votes cast on the ratification or rejection of the constitution, shall enumerate and certify the votes cast for members of Congress.[221]

This photomontage shows the "Radical members of the first legislature of South Carolina after the War." The columns of names at the bottom correspond to the descending rows of photographs running from left to right. As always, the word "Radical" means an "extreme Left-wing Liberal," and this, of course, was the very point. After expelling the legally elected white officials of South Carolina and banning former Confederate soldiers and their supporters from voting or running for political office, the North replaced the state's legislature with the men pictured here: extremely progressive white and black carpetbaggers and scallywags, individuals (many of them illiterate) who detested the white South and believed that African-Americans are superior to European-Americans. But the real purpose of these unconstitutional Reconstruction policies was not to initiate black civil rights. It was to create a fake "race war" that would upset and overturn what Liberals saw as "Southern white hegemony," a divide-and-conquer ploy still being practiced by Liberals to this day. The need for a strong Southern force to counter these illegalities was clear, and the Reconstruction KKK was the strong Southern force that answered that need.

Appendix G

"RECONSTRUCTION"
SPEECH DELIVERED TO THE CITIZENS OF
LANCASTER, PENNSYLVANIA, SEPTEMBER 7, 1865

by Thaddeus Stevens

Author's Note: Stevens, a nosy Yankee Liberal from Vermont with little knowledge of American history and absolutely no understanding of the South, was one of Dixie's most arrogant, polarizing, unrelenting, and bloodthirsty enemies, as his Lancaster speech, recorded here in its entirety, amply illustrates.

His address reveals, like nothing else could, the real "Civil War," which at its root was little more than a militaristic continuation of the ancient fight between Conservatives and Liberals; in this case, between Southern Conservatives and Northern Liberals. To make the message behind his rhetoric perfectly intelligible, Stevens' derogatory descriptions of Southerners as "rebels," "belligerents," "wretches," "enemies," "white trash," "despots," "criminals," etc., should be replaced with the word "Conservatives," while his many glowing references to Northerners should be replaced with the word "Liberals."

Steven's polemic South-hating speech, delivered in September 1865, is not only the epitome of Yankee condescension, Northern mythology, and false anti-South propaganda (some of which I have italicized), it is the clearest example of why the Reconstruction Ku Klux Klan emerged a few months later in December 1865, and why so many of its white and black members fought and even died to preserve the South over the following three years.

Had it not been for Forrest and the equally dauntless Klansmen of the Reconstruction KKK, Stevens and his aggressive Yankee meddlers would have won the "Second Civil War" (1865-1877), and there would be no American "South" today. Southerners of all races can be thankful.

FELLOW-CITIZENS: In compliance with your request, I have come to give my views of the present condition of the rebel States—of the proper mode of reorganizing the government, and the future prospects of the republic. During the whole progress of the war, I never for a moment felt doubt or despondency. I knew that the loyal North would conquer *the rebel despots who sought to destroy freedom* [it was the Confederacy which tried to preserve freedom; it was the U.S. that tried to destroy it]. But since *that traitorous confederation* has been subdued, and we have entered upon the work of "reconstruction" or "restoration," I cannot deny that my heart has become sad at the gloomy prospects before us.

Four years of *bloody and expensive war, waged against the United States by eleven States, under a government called the "Confederate States of America"* [which the South borrowed from one of the names commonly used for the original U.S.A.],²²² to which they acknowledged allegiance, have overthrown all governments within those States which could be acknowledged as legitimate by the Union. The armies of the Confederate States having been conquered and subdued, and their territory possessed by the United States, it becomes necessary to establish governments therein which shall be republican in form and principles and form a "more perfect Union" with the parent government. It is desirable that such a course should be pursued as to exclude from those governments every vestige of human bondage, and render the same forever impossible in this nation; and to take care that no principles of self-destruction shall be incorporated therein. In effecting this, it is to be hoped that no provision of the constitution

Radical Republican (then a Liberal), Pennsylvania Congressman, and bombastic South-loather, Thaddeus Stevens.

will be infringed, and no principle of the law of nations disregarded. Especially must we take care that in rebuking *this unjust and treasonable war*, the authorities of the Union shall indulge in no acts of usurpation which may tend to impair the stability and permanency of the nation. Within these limitations, *we hold it to be the duty of the government to inflict condign punishment on the rebel belligerents, and so weaken their hands that they can never again endanger the Union*; and so reform their municipal institutions as to make them republican in spirit as well as in name.

We especially insist that the property of the chief rebels should be seized and appropriated to the payment of the National debt, caused by the unjust and wicked war which they instigated [in reality, Lincoln purposefully tricked the Confederacy into firing the first shot of the War so that the South would forever bear the burden of "starting the War"].[223]

How can such punishments be inflicted and such forfeitures produced without doing violence to established principles?

Two positions have been suggested.

First—*To treat those States as never having been out of the Union because the Constitution forbids secession* [there is absolutely nothing in the Constitution that "forbids secession"; in fact, it is tacitly permitted by the Ninth and Tenth Amendments], *and therefore, a fact forbidden by law could not exist.*[224]

Second—To accept the position to which they placed themselves as severed from the Union; an independent government *de facto*, and *an alien enemy to be dealt with according to the laws of war.*

It seems to me that while we do not aver that the United States are bound to treat them as an alien enemy, yet they have a right to elect so to do if it be for the interests of the Nation; and that the "Confederate States" are estopped from denying that position. South Carolina, the leader and embodiment of the rebellion, in the month of January, 1861, passed the following resolution by the unanimous vote of her Legislature:

> "Resolved, That the separation of South Carolina from the federal Union is final, and she has no further interest in the Constitution of the United States; and that the only appropriate negotiations between her and the federal Government are as to their mutual relations as foreign States."

The convention that formed the Government of the Confederate States, and all the eleven States that composed it, adopted the same declaration, and pledged their lives and fortunes to support it. *That government raised large armies* [but only in response to Lincoln's unconstitutional order that 75,000 U.S. troops be sent to invade the South] and by its formidable power compelled the nations of the civilized world as well as our own government to acknowledge them as an independent belligerent, entitled by the law of nations to be considered as engaged in a public war, and not merely in an insurrection. It is idle to deny that we treated them as a belligerent, entitled to all the rights, and subject to all the liabilities of an alien enemy. We blockaded their ports [illegally], which is an undoubted belligerent right; the extent of coast blockaded marked the acknowledged extent of their territory—*a territory criminally acquired* but *de facto* theirs. We acknowledged their sea-rovers as privateers [illegal], and not as pirates, by ordering their captive crews to be treated as prisoners of war. We acknowledged that a commission from the Confederate Government was sufficient to screen [Confederate Read Admiral Raphael] Semmes and his associates from the fate of lawless buccaneers. Who but an acknowledged government *de jure* or *de facto*, could have power to issue such a commission? *The invaders of the loyal States* [the South did not "invade" the Northern states; the Northern states "invaded" the Southern states] were not treated as outlaws, but as soldiers of war, because they were commanded by officers holding commissions from that government. The Confederate States were for four years what they claimed to be, an alien enemy, in all their rights and liabilities. To say that they were States under the protection of *that constitution which they were rending* [the South sought to preserve the Constitution], and within the Union which they were assaulting with bloody defeats, simply because *they became belligerents through crime*, is making theory overrule fact to an absurd degree. It will, I suppose, at least be conceded that the United States, if not obliged so to do, have a right to treat them as an alien enemy, now conquered, and *subject to all the liabilities of a vanquished foe.*

If we are also at liberty to treat them as never having been out of the Union, and that their declarations and acts were all void because they contravened the constitution [false], and therefore they were never engaged in a public war, but were merely insurgents [false], let us inquire which position is best for the United States. If they have never been otherwise than States in the Union, and *we desire to try certain of the leaders for treason*, the constitution requires that they should be indicted and tried "by an impartial jury of the State and district wherein the crime shall have been committed, which district shall have been previously ascertained by law."

The crime of treason can be committed only where the person is actually or potentially present. Jefferson Davis, sitting in Richmond, counseling, or advising, or commanding an inroad into Pennsylvania, has committed no overt act in this State, and can be tried, if anywhere, only in the Richmond District. The doctrine of constructive presence, and constructive treason, will never, I hope, pollute our statutes or judicial decisions. Select an impartial jury from Virginia, and it is obvious that no conviction could ever be had. Possibly a jury might be packed to convict, but that would not be an "impartial" jury. It would be judicial murder, and would rank in infamy with the trial of Lord Russell, except only that the one was the murder of an innocent man, *the other of a traitor*. The same difficulties would exist in attempting forfeitures, which can only follow conviction in States protected by the constitution; and then it is said only for the life of the malefactor. Congress can pass no "bill of attainder."

Nor, under that theory, has Congress, much less the Executive, any power to interfere in remodeling those States upon reconstruction. What reconstruction is needed? Here are States which they say have never been out of the Union, and which are, consequently, now in it without asking leave of any one. They are competent to send Senators and members to Congress. The state of war has broken no constitutional ligaments, for it was only an insurrection of individuals, not a public war waged by States [false: it was a War between two countries, or two confederacies, to be more precise, the U.S. Confederacy and the C.S. Confederacy]. Such is the reasoning, notwithstanding every State acted in its municipal capacity; and the court in the prize cases say: "Hence in organizing this rebellion they have acted as States." It is no loose, unorganized rebellion, having no defined boundary or possession. It has a boundary, marked by lines of bayonets, and which can be crossed only by force—south of this line is enemy's territories, because it is claimed and held in possession by an organized, hostile and belligerent power. What right has any one to direct a convention to be held in a sovereign State of this Union, to amend its constitution and prescribe the qualifications of voters? The sovereign power of the nation is lodged in Congress. Yet where is the warrant in the constitution for such sovereign power, much less in the Executive, to intermeddle with the domestic institutions of a State, mould its laws, and regulate the elective franchise? It would be rank, dangerous and deplorable usurpation. In reconstruction, therefore, no reform can be effected in the Southern States if they have never left the Union. But reformation must be effected; *the foundation of their institutions, both political, municipal and social, must be broken up and relaid, or all our blood and treasure have been spent in vain.* This can only be done by treating and holding them as a compared people. *Then all things which we can desire to do, follow with logical and legitimate authority.* As conquered territory, Congress would have full power to legislate for them; for the territories are not under the constitution, except so far as the express power to govern them is given to Congress. They would be held in a territorial condition until they are fit to form State Constitutions, republican in fact, not in form only, and ask admission into the Union as new States. If Congress approve of their constitutions, and think they have done works meet for repentance, they would be admitted as new States. If their constitutions are not approved of, they would be sent back, *until they have become wise enough so to purge their old laws as to eradicate every despotic and revolutionary principle -- until they shall have learned to venerate the Declaration of Independence.* I do not touch on the question of negro suffrage. If in the Union, the States have long ago regulated that, and for the Central Government to interfere with it would be mischievous impertinence. If they are to be admitted as new States they must form their own constitution; and no enabling act could dictate its terms. Congress could prescribe the qualifications of voters while a Territory, or when proceeding to call a convention to form a State government. That is the extent of the power of Congress over the elective franchise, whether in a Territorial or State condition. The President has not even this or any other power to meddle in the subject, except by advice to Congress—and they on Territories. *Congress, to be sure, has some sort of compulsory power by refusing the States admission until they shall have complied with its wishes over this subject.* Whether those who have fought our battles should all be allowed to vote, or only those of a paler hue, I leave to be discussed in the future when Congress can take legitimate cognizance of it.

If capital punishments of the most guilty are deemed essential as examples, we have seen that, on one theory, none of them can be convicted on fair trials—the complicity of the triers would defeat it. But, as *a conquered enemy*, they could not escape. *Their trials would take place by courts-martial.* I do not think they could thus be tried for treason; but *they could be tried as belligerents, who had forfeited their lives, according to the laws of war.* By the strict rights of war, as anciently practiced, the victor held the lives, the liberty and the property of the vanquished at his disposal. The taking of the life, or reduction to bondage of the captives, have long ceased to be practiced in case of ordinary wars, but the abstract right—*the summum jus* is still recognized in exceptional cases where the cause of the war, or the character of the belligerent, or the safety of the victors justify its exercise. The same thing may be said of the seizure of property on land. [Henry W.] Halleck says some modern writers—Hautefeuille, for example—contends for the ancient rule, "that private property on land may be subject to seizure. They are undoubtedly correct, with regard to the general abstract right, as deduced from the law of nature and ancient practice." [Emer de] Vattel says: "When, therefore, he has subdued a hostile nation, he undeniably may, in the first place, do himself justice respecting the object which has given rise to the war, and indemnify himself for the expenses and damages which he has sustained by it." And at page 369: "A conqueror, who has taken up arms not only against the sovereign but against the nation herself, and whose intention it was to subdue a fierce and savage people, and once for all to reduce an obstinate enemy, such a conqueror may, with justice, lay burdens on the conquered nation, both as a compensation for the expenses of the war, and as a punishment."

I am happy to believe that the government has come to this conclusion. I cannot otherwise see how [Confederate] Capt. [Henry] Wirz can be tried by a court-martial at Washington for acts done by him at Andersonville. He was in no way connected with our military organization, nor did he as a citizen connect himself with our army so as to bring his case within any of the acts of Congress. If he committed murder in Georgia, and Georgia was a state in the Union, then he should be tried according to her laws. The General Government has no jurisdiction over such crime, and *the trial and execution of this wretch* by a United States military court would be illegal. But if he was an officer of a belligerent enemy, making war as an independent people, now being conquered, it is a competent, holding them as a conquered foe, to try him for doing acts contrary to the laws of war, and if found guilty to execute or otherwise punish him [Wirz, though obviously innocent, was later illegally executed by the U.S. government]. As I am sure the loyal man at the head of the [U.S.] government [President Andrew Johnson] will not involve the nation in illegal acts and thus set a precedent injurious to our national character, I am glad to believe that hereafter we shall treat the enemy as conquered, and remit their condition and reconstruction to the sovereign power of the nation.

In short, *all writers agree that the victor may inflict punishment upon the vanquished enemy, even to the taking of his life, liberty, or the confiscation of all his property; but that this extreme right is never exercised except upon a cruel, barbarous, obstinate, or dangerous foe who has waged an unjust war.*

Upon the character of the belligerent, and the justice of the war, and the manner of conducting it, depends our right to take the lives, liberty and property of the belligerent. *This war had its origin in treason without one spark of justice* [false]. *It was prosecuted before notice of it, by robbing our forts and armories, and our navy-yards* [false]; *by stealing our money from the mints and depositories, and by surrendering our forts and navies by perjurers who had sworn to support the constitution. In its progress our prisoners, by the authority of the government, were slaughtered in cold blood* [false]. *Ask Fort Pillow*[225] *and Fort Wagner. Sixty thousand of our prisoners have been deliberately starved to death because they would not enlist in the rebel armies* [false]. *The graves at Andersonville have each an accusing tongue. The purpose and avowed object of the enemy "to found an empire whose corner-stone should be slavery"* [this sentence was never uttered by any Southerner],[226] *rendered its perpetuity or revival dangerous to human liberty.*

Surely, these things are sufficient to justify the exercise of the extreme rights of war—"to execute, to imprison, to confiscate." *How many captive enemies it would be proper to execute, as an example to nations, I leave others to judge. I am not fond of sanguinary punishments, but surely some victims must propitiate the manes of our starved, murdered, slaughtered martyrs.* A court-martial could do justice according to law.

But *we propose to confiscate all the estate of every rebel belligerent whose estate was worth $10,000, or whose land exceeded two hundred acres in quantity*. Policy if not justice would require that the poor, the ignorant, and the coerced should be forgiven. They followed the example and teachings of their wealthy and intelligent neighbors. The rebellion would never have originated with them. *Fortunately those who would thus escape, form a large majority of the people*, though possessing but a small portion of the wealth. The proportion of those exempt compared with the punished would be I believe about nine-tenths.

There are about six millions of freedmen in the South [the true figure was closer to 4 million]. The number of acres of land is 465,000,000. Of this, those who own above two hundred acres each number about 70,000 persons, holding, in the aggregate, (together with the States,) about 394,000,000 acres, leaving for all the others below 200 each about 71,000,000 acres. *By thus forfeiting the estates of the leading rebels, the government would have 394,000,000 of acres, beside their town property, and yet nine-tenths of the people would remain untouched. Divide this land into convenient farms. Give, if you please, forty acres to each adult male freedmen. Suppose there are one million of them. That would require 40,000,000 of acres, which, deducted from 394,000,000, leaves 354,000,000 of acres for sale. Divide it into suitable farms, and sell it to the highest bidders.* I think it, including town property, would average at least $10 per acre. That would produce $3,540,000,000—three billions five hundred and forty millions of dollars.

Let that be applied as follows to wit:

1. Invest $300,000,000 in six per cent government bonds, and add the interest semi-annually to the pensions of those who have became entitled by this villainous war.

2. Appropriate $200,000,000 to pay the damages done to loyal men, North and South, by the rebellion.

3. Pay the residue, being $3,040,000,000 towards the payment of the National debt.

What loyal man can object to this? Look around you, and every where behold your neighbors, some with an arm, some with a leg, some with an eye, carried away by rebel bullets. Others horribly mutilated in every form. And yet numerous others wearing the weeds which mark the death of those on whom they leaned for support. Contemplate these monuments of rebel perfidy, and of patriotic suffering, and then say if too much is asked for our valiant soldiers.

Look again, and see loyal men reduced to poverty by the confiscations by the Confederate States, and by the rebel States—see Union men robbed of their property, and their dwellings laid in ashes by rebel raiders, and say if too much is asked for them. But, above all, let us inquire whether imperative duty to the present generation and to posterity, does not command us to compel the wicked enemy to pay the expenses of this unjust war. In ordinary transactions, he who raises a false clamor, and prosecutes an unfounded suit, is adjudged to pay the costs on his defeat. We have seen that, by the law of nations, the vanquished in an unjust war must pay the expense.

Our war debt is estimated at from three to four billions of dollars. In my judgment, when all is funded, and the pensions capitalized, it will reach more than four billions.

The interest at 6 per cent., only (now much more): $240,000,000.

The ordinary expenses of our government are $120,000,000.

For some years the extraordinary expenses of our army and navy will be $110,000,000. Total: $470,000,000.

Four hundred and seventy millions to be raised by taxation—our present heavy taxes will not, in ordinary years, produce but little more than half that sum. Can our people bear double their present taxation? He who unnecessarily causes it will be accursed from generation to generation. It is fashionable to belittle our public debt, lest the people should become alarmed, and political parties should suffer. I have never found it wise to deceive the people. They can always be trusted with *the truth*. Capitalists will not be affected, for they cannot be deceived. Confide in the people, and you will avoid repudiation. Deceive them, and lead them into false measures, and you may produce it.

We pity the poor Englishman whose national debt and burdensome taxation we have heard deplored from our childhood. The debt of Great Britain is just about as much as ours, ($4,000,000,000) four billions. But in effect it is but half as large—it bears but three per cent. interest. The current year, the Chancellor of the Exchequer tells us, the interest was $131,806,990. Ours, when all shall be funded, will be nearly double.

The plan we have proposed would pay at least three-fourths of our debt. The balance could be managed with our present taxation. And yet to think that even that is to be perpetual is sickening. If it is to be doubled, as it must be, if "restoration" instead of "reconstruction" is to prevail, would to God the authors of it could see themselves as an execrating public and posterity will see them.

Our new doctors of national law, who hold that the "Confederate States" were never out of the Union, but only insurgents and traitors, have became wiser than [Hugo] Grotius, and [Samuel von] Pufendorf, and Rutherford, and Vattel, and all modern publicists down to Halleck and [Sir Robert] Phillimore. They all agree that *such a state of things as has existed here for four years is public war, and constitutes the parties independent belligerents, subject to the same rules of war as foreign nations engaged in open warfare.*

The learned and able professor at law in the Cambridge University, Theophilus Parsons, lately said in a public speech:

"As we are victorious in war we have a right to impose upon the defeated party any terms necessary for our security. This right is perfect. It is not only in itself obvious, but it is asserted in every book on this subject, and is illustrated by all the wars of history. *The rebels forced a war upon us* [false: before and during the War the South repeatedly stated that it only wanted to be "left alone," and that it had no interest in conquering and ruling either the Northern states or the U.S. government]; *it was a long and costly and bloody war; and now that we have conquered them, we have all the rights which victory confers.*"

The only argument of the Restorationist is, that *the States could not and did not go out of the Union because the Constitution forbids it* [secession was legal then, and still is]. By the same reasoning you could prove that no crime ever existed. No man ever committed murder for the law forbids it! He is a shallow reasoner who could make theory overrule feet!

I prefer to believe the ancient and modern publicists, and the learned professors of legal science, to the extemporized doctrines of modern sciolists.

If "Restoration," as it is now properly christened, is to prevail over "Reconstruction," will some learned pundit of that school inform me in what condition slavery and the slave laws are? I assert that upon that theory not a slave has been liberated, not a slave law has been abrogated, but on the "Restoration" the whole slave code is in legal force. Slavery was protected by our constitution in every State in the Union where it existed. While they remained under that protection no power in the federal Government could abolish slavery. If, however, the Confederate States were admitted to be what they claimed, an independent belligerent *de facto*, then the war broke all treaties, compacts and ties between the parties, and slavery was left to its rights under the law of nations. These rights were none; for the law declares that "Man can hold no property in man." Then the laws of war enabled us to declare every bondman free, so long as we held them in military possession. And the conqueror, through Congress, may declare them forever emancipated. But if the States are "States in the Union," then when war ceases they resume their positions with all their privileges untouched. There can be no "mutilated" restoration. That would be the work of Congress alone, and would be "Reconstruction."

While I hear it said everywhere that slavery is dead, I cannot learn who killed it. *No thoughtful man has pretended that Lincoln's proclamation, so noble in sentiment, liberated a single slave. It expressly excluded from its operation all those within our lines. No slave within any part of the rebel States in our possession, or in Tennessee, but only those beyond our limits and beyond our power were declared free* [very true]. So Gen. Smith conquered Canada by a proclamation! The President [Lincoln] did not pretend to abrogate the slave laws of any of the States. "Restoration," therefore, will leave the "Union as it was—a hideous idea. I am aware that a very able and patriotic gentleman, and learned historian, Mr. [George] Bancroft, has attempted to place their freedom on different grounds. He says, what is undoubtedly true, that the proclamation of freedom did not free a slave. But he liberates them on feudal principles. Under the feudal system, when a king conquered his enemy, he parceled out his lands and conquered subjects among his chief retainers; the lands and serfs were held on condition of fealty and rendering military service when required. If the subordinate chief rebelled, he broke the condition on which he held them, and the lands and serfs became forfeited to the Lord paramount. But it did not free the serfs. They, with the manors, were bestowed on other favorites. But the analogy fails in another important respect. The American slaveholder does not hold, by virtue of any grant from any Lord paramount—least of all by a grant from the General Government. Slavery exists by no law of the Union, but simply by local laws, by the laws of the States. Rebellion against the National authority is a breach of no condition of their tenure. It were more analogous to say that rebellion against a State under whose laws they held, might work a forfeiture. But rebellion against neither government would per se have any such effect. On whom would the Lord paramount again bestow the slaves? The theory is plausible, but has no solid foundation.

The President says to the rebel States: "Before you can participate in the government you must abolish slavery and reform your election laws." That is the command of a conqueror. That is reconstruction, not restoration—reconstruction too by assuming the powers of Congress. This theory will lead to melancholy results. Nor can the constitutional amendment abolishing slavery ever be ratified by three-fourths of the States, if they are States to be counted. Bogus conventions of those States may vote for it. But no convention honestly and fairly elected will ever do it. The frauds will not permanently avail. The cause of liberty must rest on a firmer basis. *Counterfeit governments, like the Virginia, Louisiana, Tennessee, Mississippi and Arkansas pretenses, will be disregarded by the sober sense of the people, by future law, and by the courts.* "Restoration" is replanting the seeds of rebellion, which, within the next quarter of a century will germinate and produce the same bloody strife which has just ended.

But, it is said, by those who have more sympathy with rebel wives and children than for the widows and orphans of loyal men, that this stripping the rebels of their estates and driving them to exile or to honest labor, would be harsh and severe upon the innocent women and children. It may be so; but that is the result of the necessary laws of war. But it is revolutionary, say they. This plan would, no doubt, work a radical reorganization in Southern institutions, habits and manners. It is intended to revolutionize their principles and feelings. This may startle feeble minds and shake weak nerves. So do all great improvements in the political and moral world. It requires a heavy impetus to drive forward a sluggish people. When it was first proposed to free the slaves and arm the blacks, did not the nation tremble? The prim conservatives, the snobs, and the male waiting-maids in Congress, were in hysterics.

The whole fabric of Southern society must be changed, and never can it be done if this opportunity is lost. Without this, this government can never be, as it never has been, a true republic. Heretofore, it had more the features of aristocracy than of democracy. The Southern States have been despotisms, not governments of the people [false]. *It is impossible that any practical equality of rights can exist where a few thousand men monopolize the whole landed property* [this was not the condition in the Old South]. The larger the number of small proprietors the more safe and stable the government. As the landed interest must govern, the more it is subdivided and held by independent owners, the better. What would be the condition of the State of New-York if it were not for her independent yeomanry? She would be overwhelmed and demoralized by the Jews [Yankee anti-Semitism], Milesians and vagabonds of licentious cities. How can republican institutions, free schools, free churches, free social intercourse, exist in a mingled community of nabobs and serfs: of *the owners of twenty thousand acre manors with lordly palaces, and the occupants of narrow huts inhabited by "low white trash"?* If the South is ever to be made a safe republic, let her lands be cultivated by the toil of the owners, or the free labor of intelligent citizens. *This must be done even though it drive her nobility into exile. It they go, all the better. It will be hard to persuade the owner of ten thousand acres of land, who drives a coach and four, that he is not degraded by sitting at the same table, or in the same pew, with the embrowned and hard-handed farmer who has himself cultivated his own thriving homestead of one hundred and fifty acres* [false]. This subdivision of the lands will yield ten bales of cotton to one that is made now, and he who produced it will own it and feel himself a man.

It is far easier and more beneficial to exile 70,000 proud, bloated and defiant rebels, than to expatriate four millions of laborers, native to the soil and loyal to the government. This latter scheme was a favorite plan of the Blairs [Francis P. Blair Sr., Francis P. Blair Jr. and Montgomery Blair], with which they had for a while inoculated our late sainted President [Lincoln]. But a single experiment made him discard it and its advisers. Since I have mentioned the Blairs, I may say a word more of these persistent apologists of the South. For, *when the virus of slavery has once entered the veins of the slaveholder, no subsequent effort seems capable of wholly eradicating it* [false: the American abolition movement started in the South].[227] *They are a family of Considerable power, some merit, of admirable audacity and execrable selfishness* [false: Southern slave owners registered their servants as literal family members at the time of purchase].[228] *With impetuous alacrity they seize the White House, and hold possession of it, as in the late administration, until shaken off by the overpowering force of public indignation. Their pernicious counsel had well nigh defeated the reelection of Abraham Lincoln* [false: Lincoln ran on a platform that promised "not to interfere" with slavery and he supported the 1865 Corwin Amendment, which would have allowed slavery to continue in perpetuity][229]: *and if it should prevail with the present administration, pure and patriotic as President Johnson admitted to be, it will render him the most unpopular Executive—saves one—that ever occupied the Presidential chair.* But there is no fear of that. He will soon say, as Mr. Lincoln did: "Your time has come!"

This remodeling the institutions, and reforming the rooted habits of a proud aristocracy, is undoubtedly a formidable task, requiring the broad mind of enlarged statesmanship, and the firm nerve of the hero. But will not this mighty occasion produce—will not the God of liberty and order give us—such men? Will not a Romulus, a Lycurgus, a Charlemagne, a Washington arise, whose expansive views will found a free empire, to endure till time shall be no more?

This doctrine of Restoration shocks me. We have a duty to perform which our fathers were incapable of, which will be required at our hands by God and our country. When our ancestors found a "more perfect Union" necessary, they found it impossible to agree upon a constitution without tolerating, nay, guaranteeing, slavery. They were obliged to acquiesce, trusting to time to work a speedy cure, in which they were disappointed. They had some excuse, some justification. But we can have none if we do not thoroughly eradicate slavery and render it forever impossible in this republic. *The slave power made war upon the nation* [false]. *They declared the "more perfect Union" dissolved—solemnly declared themselves a foreign nation, alien to this republic; for four years were in fact what they claimed to be. We accepted the war which they tendered and treated them as a government capable of making war. We have conquered them, and as a conquered enemy we can give them laws; can abolish all their municipal institutions and form now ones. If we do not make those institutions fit to last through generations of freemen, a heavy curse will be on us. Our glorious but tainted republic has been born to new life through bloody, agonizing pains. But this frightful "Restoration" has thrown it into "cold obstruction, and to death." If the rebel States have never been out of the Union, any attempt to reform their State institutions, either by Congress or the President, is rank usurpation.*

Is then all lost? Is this great conquest to be in vain? That will depend upon the virtue and intelligence of the next Congress. To Congress alone belongs the power of reconstruction—of giving law to the vanquished. This is expressly declared by the Supreme Court of the United States in the Dorr case. The court says, "Under this article of the constitution (the 4th) it rests with Congress to decide what government is the established one in a State, for the United States guarantees to each a republican form of government," etc. But we know how difficult it is for a majority of Congress to overcome preconceived opinions. Besides, before Congress meets, things will be so inaugurated—precipitated—it will be still more difficult to correct. If a majority of Congress can be found wise and firm enough to declare the Confederate States a conquered enemy, reconstruction will be easy and legitimate; and *the friends of freedom* will long rule in the councils of the nation. If restoration prevails the prospect is gloomy, and the new "lords will make new laws." The Union [Liberal] party will be overwhelmed. *The Copperhead party has become extinct with secession* [false: there are still thousands of Copperheads to this day]. But with succession it will revive. Under "restoration" every rebel State will send rebels to Congress, and they, with their allies in the North, will control Congress, and occupy the White House. Then restoration of laws and ancient constitutions will be sure to follow, our public debt will be repudiated, or the rebel national debt will be added to ours, and the people be crushed beneath heavy burdens [false].

Let us forget all parties, and build on the broad platform of "reconstructing" the government out of the conquered territory converted into new and free States, and admitted into the Union by the sovereign power of Congress, with another plank—*"The property of the rebels shall pay our national debt, and indemnify freedmen and loyal sufferers—and that under no circumstances will we suffer the national debt to be repudiated, or the interest scaled below the contract rates; nor permit any part of the rebel debt to be assumed by the nation."*

Let all who approve of these principles rally with us. Let all others go with Copperheads and rebels. Those will be the opposing parties. Young men, this duty devolves on you. Would to God, if only for that, that I were still in the prime of life, that I might aid you to fight through this last and greatest battle of freedom![230]

This drawing commemorates a glorious day in the history of Louisiana: the withdrawal of the last Federal troops from the state on April 24, 1877, permanently ending Reconstruction and its much hated Liberal anti-South polices.

Appendix H

THE STORY OF THE KU KLUX KLAN:
SOME OF ITS LEADERS, LIVING & DEAD

by Thomas Dixon Jr.

From *The Metropolitan Magazine*, September 1905, Vol. 22, No. 6

The Northern conception of the Ku Klux Klan is voiced in a recent criticism of my last novel by an ancient Boston newspaper thus:

> He reaches the acme of his sectional passions when he exalts the Ku Klux Klan into an association of Southern patriots, when he must know, or else be strangely ignorant of American history, that its members were as arrant ruffians, desperadoes and scoundrels as ever went unhanged.

If this be true, moral miracles have been wrought by ruffians, desperadoes and scoundrels which require study. The like of it has never been recorded in the history of the race, and if such things were done by scoundrels the basis of ethics must be rebuilt by our philosophers.

. . . The Ku Klux Klan was a great Law and Order League of mounted night cavalrymen called into action by the intolerable conditions of a reign of terror under Negro rule in the South. It was the answer to their foes of an indomitable race of men, conquered, betrayed, disarmed and driven to desperation. It was the old answer of organized manhood to organized crime masquerading under the forms of government.

Its rise was due to the mind of no leader. It was an accident. It was a case of spontaneous combustion.

A group of college boys at Pulaski, Tennessee, organized it first as a local college fraternity. They found a name in the Greek work "Kuklos," a band, or circle, and to this they added Clan, and then split the germ word into two weird monosyllables, spelling the Clan with a K, to heighten the appeal to the superstitious, and lo, the awe-inspiring

"Ku Klux Klan"!

The terror of these silent ghosts, riding in the night, reduced the Negro race to an immediate and profound peace. The idea spread to an adjoining county and rapidly over the state of Tennessee which was the first to pass beneath the yoke of Negro supremacy.

In 1867 a secret convention of peaceloving, law-abiding, God-fearing, patriotic Southerners met in Nashville and organized this society into "The Invisible Empire," adopted a ritual, and adjourned. They met in the ruins of an old homestead within the picket lines of 35,000 [U.S.] troops sent there to enforce the rule of the black slave over his former master.

As the young German patriots of 1812 organized their struggle for liberty under the noses of the garrisons of Napoleon, so these daring men, girt by thousands of bayonets, discussed and adopted under the cover of darkness the ritual of "The Invisible Empire."

Within a few months this Empire had overspread a territory larger than modern Europe and brought order out of chaos. The triumph which they achieved was one of incredible grandeur. They snatched power out of defeat and death, and tore the fruits of victory from twenty million conquerors. Such achievements have never been wrought by arrant ruffians, scoundrels and desperadoes. The sheer moral grandeur of such a deed gives the lie to the assertion.

The truth of history is, that, as originally organized and led, the Ku Klux Klan was the sole guardian of civilization in the South from 1867 to 1870 and its members were the salt of the earth.

Every hope of relief for the South had been crushed. The assassination of Lincoln had so crazed the masses of the North that the Radical [that is, Liberal] wing of the [Republican] party in power could propose no outrage too monstrous for the consideration of Congress. Even a bill to tear from the starving Southern people the remnant of their property left by the war and give it to the negroes and camp followers of the army was introduced in the House of Representatives by Thaddeus Stevens, the responsible leader of the Government, and boldly championed by this great man with the audacity of genius and the faith of a fanatic.

The Negro had been made the ruler of his former master who was disfranchised and disarmed. The hand of the thief and ruffian clutched at every man's throat. The Negro controlled the state, county, city and town governments. Their insolence grew apace. Their women were taught to insult their old mistresses and mock their poverty as they passed in their faded dresses. A black driver in a town near mine, struck a white child of six with a whip, and when the mother protested she was arrested by a negro policeman and fined ten dollars by a negro magistrate for insulting a freedman!

Thieves looted the treasury of every state and county, and taxes mounted until as many as 2,900 homesteads of white men, many of whom could not vote, were sold for taxes in a single county.

The Negro and his ally the carpet-bag adventurer had attained undisputed control of society through the secret oath-hound order known as "The Union League."

The white people of the South at first scouted the idea that the negroes, who had been faithful through the war, could now be used as their deadliest foes in the new order of society. But for the signs, grip, passwords, and mysterious blue flaming altar of "The Union League," the whites could have grew rapidly into a restless political power, held the friendship of their former slaves. As a rule the ties which bound them were based on real affection. But the League did its work well. By promises to the slaves of forty acres of the land of their former masters linked with the wildest theories of equality and dominion over those who once ruled them, by drill in arms and the backing of trained garrisons, a gulf between the white man of the South and the Negro was dug which time can never bridge. Its passions have become part of the very heart beat of both races.

The Union League of America was organized in Cleveland, Ohio, during the war by the friends of Thaddeus Stevens, the Radical leader of Congress. Its prime object was the confiscation of the property of the South.

. . . When the time was ripe, Mr. Stevens, in 1867, destroyed the state governments in the South which had been established by President [Andrew] Johnson, permitting the former slave to vote to enfranchise himself and disfranchise his master at the same election. He divided the territory from the James [River in Virginia] to the Rio Grande [in Texas] into five military satrapies and sent the [U.S.] armies back into the South to enforce compliance with Negro rule. In short, he placed a ballot in the hands of every negro and a bayonet at the breast of every white man.

The South felt that no people had ever been so basely betrayed or so wantonly humiliated.

Judge Albion W. Tourgee, author of *A Fool's Errand*, which is the carpet-bagger's story of the Klan, pays a tribute in this book to the organizers of the "Invisible Empire," which is very remarkable, when we remember that he was writing of enemies who had on more than one occasion sought his life. He says:

> Such, however, was the indomitable spirit of the Southern people that they scorned to yield to what they deemed oppression, protesting with indignation, denouncing with rage and fiercely submitting almost with tears. No conquered foe ever passed under the yoke, which they conceived to mean servitude and infamy with more unwilling step or more deeply muttered curses. The Ku Klux Order was a daring conception for a conquered people. Only a race of warlike instincts and regal pride could have conceived or executed it. Men, women and children must have, and be worthy of, implicit mutual trust. They must be trusted with the secrets of life and death without reserve and without fear. It was a magnificent conception and in a sense deserved success. It differed from all other attempts at revolution in the caution and skill with which it required to be conducted. It was a movement made in the face of the enemy, and an enemy of overwhelming strength. Should it succeed it would be the most brilliant revolution ever accomplished. Should it fail—well, those who engaged in it felt that they had nothing more to lose.

Judge Tourgee was in my opinion the most brilliant carpet-bagger who found fame and fortune in the ruined South. In many ways he was a remarkable man. His death was decreed by the Ku Klux Klan for the part he took in persuading Governor [William W.] Holden to suspend the writ of *Habeas Corpus* in North Carolina. The writ had never been suspended for a moment during the entire history of the Commonwealth, not even during the four years of war when the conscript acts were enforced. A hundred picked men were commissioned to execute Tourgee and the Governor for this usurpation of power and throw their bodies into the Capital Square at Raleigh. They failed only because of a warning received in time. And yet this big-brained, self-poised Yankee sat down afterwards and wrote the tribute to his foes I quote. We Southerners are much too intense in our feelings to do such things.

It never occurred to Judge Tourgee at the time he wrote this book that the members of this Klan were merely a set of scoundrels and desperadoes [as our enemies label them].

. . . When the reign of terror which followed Negro rule reached its climax as many as nine burning barns were seen at one time from the Court House Square of the town of Dallas in Gaston County, North Carolina.

Taxpayer conventions met and appealed to Washington in vain. The Administration answered by sending more rifles to arm the Negro militia.

The laws forbidding the intermarriage of races were repealed by military proclamation and the commanding General of North Carolina took a negro woman with him over the state in a special car and made speeches from the platform, declaring that she was his wife, that a new era had dawned in the history of the world, and that he was there to enforce its spirit with the bayonet if need be.

. . . In this the darkest hour of the life of the South, and the lowest in public morals ever known in the Nation, the Invisible Empire suddenly rose from the field of death and challenged the visible to mortal combat.

Within a few months after the appearance of the white brotherhood, the disorders of anarchy were succeeded by a strange peace, positively weird in its completeness, according to the acknowledgment of Judge Tourgee. In the first campaign they overturned the Negro governments of six Southern states, and the others, one by one, were redeemed under the inspiration of this success.

In North Carolina, my uncle, Colonel Leroy McAfee, was elected to the Legislature from Cleveland County and as the representative of the Klan on the Judiciary Committee, impeached Governor Holden, removed him from office and deprived him of his citizenship.

. . . When Colonel McAfee returned from the Legislature after the overthrow of the Reconstruction government, he disbanded the Ku Klux Klan in his district in accordance with General Forrest's orders. Younger and more desperate men reorganized it as a local fraternity to their own sorrow and the disgrace of some sections of our mountain region. Its degeneracy into fierce neighborhood feuds and its perversion by the lawless swiftly followed until it became necessary for the organizers of the original Klan to aid in the suppression of its spurious successors.

My father, Rev. Thomas Dixon, Sr., was a member of the original Klan under Colonel McAfee's leadership and aided him in the suppression of its reckless imitators. He was preeminently the type of man whose name made the Klan a resistless power the first two years of its existence. He never attended a meeting of the order or took any active part in its work, except as an elder counseller of wisdom and moderation to its chosen leaders, but his name was a tower of strength. He is and always was a man of peace and a lover of order. He saw the war begin with infinite sorrow. He is a man of large patriotic views, though an ardent Southerner. He comes of the stock that created this Republic. His grandfather, Lt. Colonel Frederick Hambright, was a member of the Continental Congress and commanded a regiment of Revolutionary patriots at the battle of Kings Mountain. He is to-day a venerable minister of Christ, who in a ministry of sixty years has built twenty flourishing churches in Piedmont, North Carolina. He knew and dreaded the dangerous power of a secret oath-bound political order. He went into it reluctantly. He joined with every other minister in the county, only because it was the last resort of despair to save society from the intolerable curse of Negro dominion, [Northern] insolence, and [Yankee] crime.

A study of the portrait of Thaddeus Stevens, the man who created the Union League and sent it on its mission of revenge and confiscation, and the face of my father may settle the question as to which of the two was the "desperado" of this stirring drama. In the one is seen the grim soul of a cynic and misanthrope, audacity in every line of his magnificent head, and merciless cruelty in his terrible mouth. In the other patience, good humor and boundless faith in God and man. Let the reader of these two faces pick the "ruffian" of the two.

But for Mr. Stevens there never would have been a Union League, and but for the Union League there never would have been a Ku Klux Klan.

. . . The order of dissolution of the Klan as issued by General Forrest was in every way characteristic of the man. When the white race had redeemed six Southern States from Negro rule in 1870, the Grand Wizard knew that his mission was accomplished and issued at once his order to disband. The execution of this command by young [John W.] Morton the Cyclops of the Nashville Den, also of the staff of the Grand Wizard, is typical of what occurred throughout the South.

Thirty-five picked men, mounted, armed and in full Ku Klux regalia for both horses and men, were selected for the ceremony, and ordered to boldly parade through the streets of Nashville. The Capitol was still in charge of 3,000 Reconstruction Militia and 200 metropolitan police who had sworn to take every Ku Klux Klansman dead or alive who dared to show himself abroad.

On the night appointed, the squadron of thirty-five white and scarlet horsemen moved out of the woods and bore down upon the city. The streets were soon crowded with people watching the strange procession of ghostlike figures. On the principal streets the police blew their whistles and darted here and there in great excitement, but made no move to stop the dare-devil paraders. On they rode up the hill and passed the Capitol building, round which the camp-fires of a thousand soldiers burned brightly, and not a hand was lifted against them.

They turned south into High Street and ladies began to wave their handkerchiefs from windows and men to shout and cheer from the sidewalks. The scalawag police received these shouts with suppressed oaths. At last they began to summon citizens to aid in the arrest of the clansmen. The citizens laughed at them.

On reaching Broad Street, young Morton, who rode at the head of the squadron, observed a line of police drawn across the street with the evident intention of attempting to stop or arrest the riders. Turning to Mart N. Brown, a gallant clansman who rode by his side, Morton said: "What shall we do, Mart?" "Turn into Vine Street," he quickly answered, "pass around them."

"No—ride straight through them without a change of gait!" was Morton's order.

And they did. The astonished police, dumbfounded at the insolence of the raiders, opened their lines and the horsemen rode slowly through without a word.

They passed a large frame building used as a carpet-bag militia armory. It was full of negroes. Morton halted his line of white figures, drew them up at dress parade, rode up to the door and knocked. The negroes rushed to the doors and windows, and when they saw in the bright moonlight the grim figures, they forgot the police and the 3,000 soldiers guarding Nashville. They made a unanimous break for the rear, and went out through every opening without knowledge of any obstruction. Many of them wore window sash home for collars.

The clansmen silently wheeled again into double column and rode toward their old rendezvous. They had overthrown the carpet-bag Negro regime and restored civilization. Their last act was a warning. A handful of their men boldly slapped the face of the hostile authorities, before the new administration entered upon its work, and dared them lift a hand again.

Outside the city they entered the shadows of a forest. Down its dim cathedral aisles, lit by trembling threads of moonbeams, the white horsemen slowly wound their way to their appointed place. For the last time the Chaplain led in prayer, the men disrobed, drew from each horse his white mantle, opened a grave and solemnly buried their regalia, sprinkling the folds with the ashes of the copy of their burned ritual. In this weird ceremony thus ended the most remarkable revolution of history.[231]

The Atlanta, Georgia, home of William Joseph Simmons, founder of the New KKK, or Knights of the Ku Klux Klan, in 1915. The home was given to Simmons, the group's Imperial Wizard, by members of the organization.

Appendix I

PRAYER OFFERED BY DR. KENNEDY AT THE UNVEILING OF A MEMORIAL HONORING THE BIRTHPLACE OF THE KU KLUX KLAN AT PULASKI, TENNESSEE, MAY 1, 1917

Under the direction of the local chapter of the United Daughters of the Confederacy

FROM *CONFEDERATE VETERAN*, JULY 1917, VOL. 25, NO. 7

O thou God and Father of all, Sovereign of the universe, foreordaining whatsoever comes to pass for thine own glory, ordering the steps of men and determining the destinies of peoples and nations, "doing according to thy will in the army of heaven and among the inhabitants of the earth, and none can stay thy hand or say unto thee, 'What doest thou?'" we give thee honor and do thee obeisance this day as we stand on ground made historic by thy providences. By thy ordering of events what was once a humble law office has become a historic spot, and to-day we mark it as such.

The inception of a circle (a *kyklos*) of six men for pleasure and pastime, by the extension of its radii and enlargement of its circumference, grew and enlarged to encircle an organized and mobilized army profound in secrecy, startling in mystery, terrible with banners, and determined for the right.

That which at first was frightful in amusement later became gruesome in resisting oppression and restraining lawlessness for the defense of our homes. In frightful costume the slain of many battle fields apparently arose to the defense of their homes and country; the silent dead lived again, displayed their wounds, and spoke in gutteral tones of the grave; the keen thirst of the long-wounded was slaked with marvelous draughts, and men stood aghast. As a result the inflamed intruder and startled observer fled from his nefarious purposes and sought hiding places from these hosts of the grave. Thus out of innocent amusement grew a discovered power of restraint and unforeseen deliverance, an army of defense, a safeguard of virtue, and a victory for the right. Thine be the glory, Almighty God.

In recognition of thy goodness and in appreciation of the service of heroes to-day we place our marker, a merited historic tablet, upon the one, the real, the only birthplace of the Ku-Klux Klan. We do honor to thousands of men who came from dens and caves in the weird mystery of nightfall to the defense of our rights and homes and who, both horse and rider, their mission having been accomplished, disappeared into the unknown as silently and mysteriously as they came. *For the racial friendship* and the national peace which bless our homes to-day *we give thee thanks, thou God of destinies.*

Great God, by thy might protect us still. Keep us from bloody entanglement with foreign powers. Speedily bring peace to the world. Bless the youth of our land and of our various schools assembled here. Standing upon the contiguous bases of two historic spots in Pulaski, the death place of Sam Davis, the youthful hero, and the birthplace of the Ku-Klux Klan, may they catch the inspiration of the hour and imbibe the spirit of the men we honor, most of whom are dead, only a few of the Klan being present with us to-day! Give us sons and daughters *wedded to liberty, loyal to country, adherents to truth*, the soul of honor and devoted to thee. Let thy favor abide with the good women who in these exercises labor to preserve and perpetuate the history of our Southern homes and Southern chivalry. And when heroes and defenders are all dead, when the love and devotion of women shall have grown cold, when the fires of the stars of heaven shall have burned out, be thou our God and Protector still for Jesus' sake. Amen.[232]

A Confederate reunion of members of Forrest's Escort in the early 1900s at Lynchburg, Tennessee. Several of the General's black soldiers are in attendance.

Notes

1. On Lincoln's socialistic, Marxist, and communist thoughts, ideas, and tendencies, see e.g., McCarty, passim; Browder, passim; Benson and Kennedy, passim.
2. See J. W. Jones, TDMV, pp. 144, 200-201, 273.
3. See Seabrook, TAHSR, passim. See also, Pollard, LC, p. 178; J. H. Franklin, pp. 101, 111, 130, 149; Nicolay and Hay, ALCW, Vol. 1, p. 627.
4. See e.g., Seabrook, TQNBF, pp. 91, 116, 118.
5. See e.g., R. Taylor, pp. vii, 1, 2, 15, 46, 125, 296, 308, 362.
6. See e.g., Seabrook, TQNBF, p. 6.
7. See e.g., A. H. Stephens, RAHS, p. 56.
8. See e.g., Seabrook, TQJD, pp. 30, 38, 76.
9. See e.g., J. Davis, RFCG, Vol. 2, pp. 4, 161, 454, 610.
10. See e.g., Seabrook, TQJD, pp. 30, 38, 76.
11. Seabrook, EYWTATCWIW, p. 13.
12. For more on Lincoln's attitude toward African-Americans, see my books: Seabrook, ALSV, passim; Seabrook, TGI, passim; Seabrook, L, passim; and Seabrook, TUAL, passim.
13. Seabrook, TUAL, p. 91.
14. There are known exceptions to these rules.
15. The word racism, which is now more correctly called ethnosadism, remains meaningful in one sense: race-baiters who use this word to foment racial divisiveness are revealed as true "racists"; that is, these are individuals who judge others strictly by the color of their skin.
16. Anthropologists, in fact, no longer use the vague word race, which, as mentioned, has been replaced with the more scientifically accurate term ethnogroup: "a population of people who share a common origin, background, nationality, culture, descent, religion, or language."
17. We truly are one species and one "race": All humans, for example, share the same number of chromosomes and are inter-fertile, and everyone's blood is constructed of the identical pattern of agglutinins and antigens, which is what makes blood transfusions possible between all people. For more on the topic of genetics and race, see my detailed discussion in Seabrook, EYWTAASIW, pp. 14-16.
18. Horn, IE, p. 9.
19. Horn, IE, pp. 312-314.
20. Henry, FWMF, pp. 442-443. The Klan formed in late 1865; Forrest began to support it in 1867.
21. Horn, IE, p. 436.
22. Lester and Wilson, p. 26; Rogers, KKS, p. 34; Hurst, p. 305.
23. Horn, IE, pp. 362-363, 38.
24. Browning, p. 98.
25. W. Jones, pp. 57-63.
26. Horn, IE, pp. 426-439, 365-367, 369; Rose, p. 30.
27. Horn, IE, pp. 3, 26-30.
28. Horn, IE, pp. 376-377.
29. Rose, p. 28.
30. See e.g., Robuck, pp. 118-119.
31. Horn, IE, pp. 312, 36.
32. Henry, FWMF, p. 443.
33. Rose, p. 7.
34. Gordon, a cousin of mine, was captured at Fort Donelson in February 1862. See Morton, p. 363.
35. Wills, p. 336.
36. Page Smith, p. 844.
37. Horn, IE, p. 37.
38. Page Smith, p. 844.

39. Horn, IE, p. 313.
40. Wyeth, LGNBF, p. 619.
41. Sheppard, p. 289.
42. Horn, IE, pp. 315-316.
43. Morton, passim. The section in Morton's Appendix in which the subject of Forrest and the KKK are discussed was contributed by others.
44. In 1907 Rutherford wrote of *The Clansman* that it created "an unusual sensation, because at the North it opened the eyes of even the strongest abolitionist sympathizer to the suffering of the South during that period, and showed in an unanswerable way that the placing of the South under military rule, and giving free rein to the negro as yet unfitted for freedom, and establishing the Freedman's Bureau which necessitated the Ku Klux Klan were the causes that many believe have brought about the present state of unrest." Rutherford, p. 610.
45. Bradley, pp. 211-212.
46. Wyeth, LGNBF, p. 619.
47. *Report of the Joint Select Committee to Inquire into the Condition of Affairs in the Late Insurrectionary States*, p. 6.
48. Sheppard, p. 291.
49. Wyeth, LGNBF, pp. 619-620.
50. Henry, FWMF, p. 448.
51. Bradley, p. 138.
52. Jordan and Pryor, p. 208; Morton, p. 62.
53. W. L. Jones, Vol. 2, p. 174. My paraphrasal.
54. Wills, p. 320.
55. Henry, FWMF, p. 441.
56. *Report of the Joint Committee on Reconstruction, at the First Session, Thirty-ninth Congress*, p. 106.
57. Wyeth, LGNBF, p. 616.
58. Wills, pp. 320-321.
59. Henry, FWMF, p. 440.
60. *Report of the Joint Select Committee to Inquire into the Condition of Affairs in the Late Insurrectionary States*, p. 25.
61. Sheppard, p. 284. Some sources say his name was spelled Diffenbacher, or Diffenbocker, and that he was from Minnesota. See e.g., Henry, FWMF, p. 400.
62. Ashdown and Caudill, p. 55.
63. *Report of the Joint Select Committee to Inquire into the Condition of Affairs in the Late Insurrectionary States*, p. 24.
64. In fact, shortly after the War ended Forrest began welcoming Northerners into the South.
65. Sheppard, p. 284.
66. Henry, ATSF, p. 45.
67. Sheppard, p. 283.
68. Wyeth, LGNBF, p. 616; Henry, ATSF, p. 127.
69. Rose, p. 32.
70. Mathes, pp. 359-360. Edwards was known for his cruelty to animals as well. Only weeks prior to his death at Forrest's hands, the freedman had mercilessly beat a mule to death. On another occasion Edwards whipped his wife so badly that a doctor had to be called. Wills, pp. 325-326.
71. Hurst, p. 273.
72. McFeely, p. 264.
73. Hurst, p. 274.
74. Wills, p. 328.
75. Memphis *Avalanche*, April 10, 1866, p. 2.
76. Martinez, p. 20.
77. Mathes, p. 358.

78. *Report of the Joint Select Committee to Inquire into the Condition of Affairs in the Late Insurrectionary States*, p. 20.
79. Henry, FWMF, p. 441. My paraphrasal.
80. Hurst, p. 332. My paraphrasal.
81. Lytle, p. 378; Sheppard, p. 292.
82. Henry, FWMF, p. 452.
83. Mathes, p. 361.
84. *Report of the Joint Select Committee to Inquire into the Condition of Affairs in the Late Insurrectionary States*, p. 30.
85. Wills, p. 366; Hurst, 362.
86. My 4th great-grandmother is Phoebe Rucker of Orange Co., Virginia, Edmund's 1st cousin.
87. *Report of the Joint Select Committee to Inquire into the Condition of Affairs in the Late Insurrectionary States*, p. 17.
88. *Report of the Joint Select Committee to Inquire into the Condition of Affairs in the Late Insurrectionary States*, p. 17.
89. Henry, FWMF, p. 443.
90. Lytle, p. 382.
91. Sheppard, pp. 286-287.
92. Seabrook, NBF, p. 53.
93. Mathes, p. 371.
94. Mathes, pp. 368-369.
95. Bradley, p. 137.
96. R. E. Lee, Jr., pp. 347-348.
97. J. Davis, Vol. 2, p. 732.
98. See Seabrook, C101, passim; Stephens, CV, Vol. 1, pp. 504-505.
99. To this day the Fourteenth Amendment, which was used by Lincoln and his Northern-controlled Congress to replace America's original Republic-style government with a Federal-style government, has still not been legally or formerly ratified. The Confederacy understandably rejected the Fourteenth Amendment, since it transferred power from the individual sovereign states to Lincoln's new all-powerful, highly centralized government in Washington, D.C., the form in which it remains to this day. For more on why the Fourteenth Amendment was condemned across Dixie, see L. Johnson, pp. 241-242; Woods, pp. 86-90; Findlay and Findlay, pp. 228-235; DiLorenzo, RL, pp. 207-208, 211.
100. Lester and Wilson, p. 28.
101. Browning, p. 98.
102. Rose, p. 76.
103. An example of an order put out by the Reconstruction KKK, using language meant to intimidate and terrify: "Make ready! Make ready! Make ready! The mighty Hobgoblins of the Confederate Dead in a Hell a Bulloo assembled! Revenge, Revenge! Be secret, be cautious, be terrible! By special grant, Hell freezes over for your passage. Offended ghosts, put on your skates, and cross over to mother earth!" Rose, pp. 44, 48-49.
104. Rose, pp. 55-59. See also W. Jones, p. 75.
105. Rose, p. 27.
106. Seabrook, TMCP, p. 163.
107. Rose, pp. 25, 77.
108. W. T. Richardson, p. 8.
109. *Reports of the Committees of the Senate of the United States (for the Second Session of the Forty-second Congress)*, p. 33.
110. Damer, p. 93. This quote is a paraphrasal by the author Eyre Damer.
111. Rose, pp. 40-41. Emphasis added.
112. Rose, p. 41.
113. Rose, pp. 41-42.

114. Marchmont, p. 263. Emphasis added.
115. Morton, p. 343; Horwitz, pp. 200-201.
116. See e.g., Fry, p. 171.
117. Fry, p. 99. Emphasis added.
118. For more on this topic, see Seabrook, EYWTATCWIW, passim; Seabrook, EYWTAASIW, passim; Seabrook, TGYC, passim; Seabrook, CCF, passim.
119. Lester and Wilson, p. 26; Rogers, p. 34; Browning, p. 103; Hurst, p. 305.
120. Some of these Southern blacks suffered torture and even death for their loyalty to the South and the Reconstruction KKK. See e.g., W. Jones, p. 75.
121. Rose, p. 56.
122. Horn, IE, pp. 362-363. We will note that at one time (1920s-1930s) even the modern KKK—though it has no connection with the original KKK—possessed African-American members, and treated both whites and blacks the same. Terkel, p. 239. In Indiana, for example, after white klansmen decided they wanted to broaden their racial base, they organized a "colored division" whose uniforms were white capes, blue masks, and red robes. Blee, p. 169.
123. Rose, p. 51. Emphasis added.
124. See W. Jones, pp. 44-45. Emphasis added.
125. *Report of the Joint Select Committee to Inquire into the Condition of Affairs in the Late Insurrectionary States*, p. 23.
126. Fry, p. 168.
127. Fry, pp. 167-169. Emphasis added.
128. Wills, p. 350. My paraphrasal.
129. Evidence points to Minor Meriwether as Tennessee's first Grand Dragon. Page Smith, p. 844.
130. Lester and Wilson, p. 30.
131. See e.g., W. Jones, p. 75.
132. Lester and Wilson, pp. 79-80; Mathes, p. 372; Henry, FWMF, p. 443; Ridley, pp. 649-650.
133. Lester and Wilson, p. 31.
134. Browning, pp. 99-100.
135. Morton, p. 341.
136. Ashdown and Caudill, p. 62.
137. Horn, IE, pp. 356-357.
138. Morton, p. 342.
139. Morton, p. 346.
140. *Report of the Joint Select Committee to Inquire into the Condition of Affairs in the Late Insurrectionary States*, p. 16.
141. *Reports of the Committees of the Senate of the United States (for the Second Session of the Forty-second Congress)*, p. 34.
142. *Reports of the Committees of the Senate of the United States (for the Second Session of the Forty-second Congress)*, p. 34.
143. Ridley, pp. 657-658. My emphasis.
144. William Garrott Brown, "The Ku Klux Movement," *The Atlantic Monthly*, Vol. 87 (1901), p. 639.
145. For details regarding Brownlow's mishandling of the Reconstruction KKK, see W. Jones, p. 46.
146. Browning, p. 102.
147. Horn, IE, p. 104. My paraphrasal.
148. Morton, pp. 342-343.
149. W. Jones, pp. 47-48.
150. W. Jones, pp. 57-63.
151. Fry, p. 163.
152. W. Jones, p. 62.
153. Mathes, p. 373.
154. Rose, pp. 18-19.

155. Rose, pp. 34, 69. Emphasis added.
156. See e.g., W. Jones, p. 71.
157. W. Jones, pp. 69-76. Emphasis added. Of the modern KKK's attitude regarding race and membership, in the early 1900s Colonel Simmons wrote: "It is true that we bar Jews, Catholics, and negroes. These classes also bar from membership in their organizations persons who are not Jews, Catholics, or negroes. We have the same right." W. Jones, p. 80.
158. For more on my theory that Lincoln was the originator of America's nanny state, see my four Lincoln books.
159. Rose, pp. 14-17. Emphasis added.
160. Sheppard, p. 287.
161. *Report of the Joint Select Committee to Inquire into the Condition of Affairs in the Late Insurrectionary States*, pp. 453-454. See also Adams and Sanders, p. 217.
162. The second Freedmen's Bureau Bill was passed on February 6, 1866, but was vetoed by President Andrew Johnson. A third bill, passed on July 16, 1866, overturned the president's veto. A fourth bill was passed in June 1868, and the final one was passed on January 1, 1869. From the third bill on, the focus was mainly on extending the duration and powers of the earlier bills. Colby, s.v. "Freedmen's Bureau." It was shortly after this that Forrest disbanded the Reconstruction KKK—although the "educational work" of the Bureau did not officially end until January 1, 1870. Lalor, s.v. "Freedmen's Bureau, The."
163. The Fourteenth Amendment was never legally ratified, and today it remains an illegal addition to the U.S. Constitution.
164. W. Jones, pp. 13-18, 21. Emphasis added.
165. W. Jones, pp. 34-35. Emphasis added.
166. The full term "waving the bloody shirt" was a maneuver used by Liberal Yankees during and after the Civil War to remind fellow Northerners of the sacrifices made by Union soldiers in their war against the "evil South" in order to "preserve the Union and abolish slavery." Its true purpose was to whip up Northern support by inflaming sectional animosities and creating racism where it did not exist. This had the effect of maintaining the country in a state of imbalance, making it easier to control the masses. This same ploy continues to be one of the primary weapons used by Democrats, Liberals, socialists, and South-loathers in general.
167. Meriwether, pp. 220-228. Emphasis added.
168. W. Wilson, Vol. 9, pp. 46-52, 58-64. Emphasis added.
169. W. Jones, p. 69.
170. Burton, pp. 9-15. Emphasis added.
171. Fry, pp. 123-126.
172. Beard, p. 21.
173. Rose, pp. 26-28.
174. See, e.g., Highsmith and Landphair, p. 28.
175. Henry, FWMF, p. 443.
176. Rose, p. 20; Lester and Wilson, pp. 19-21. Some sources state that J. Calvin Jones' name was "Calvin E. Jones." See e.g., *Confederate Veteran*, July 1917, Vol. 25, No. 7, p. 335.
177. The first parade of the Reconstruction KKK took place on the night of July 4, 1867, at Pulaski, Tennessee. Rose, p. 46.
178. Forrest was said to have been voted in as Grand Wizard at a meeting in Room 10, in the Maxwell House Hotel (see Morton, p. 344), although there is absolutely no evidence for this assertion. Revealingly, the entry on the Maxwell House Hotel in *The Tennessee Encyclopedia of History and Culture* makes no mention of Forrest, or even of the KKK, in relation to the building, though this seems to be what it was most famous for right up into the present day. Indeed, when the Maxwell House Hotel burned down in 1961, many believed that it was most likely the victim of arson due to its associations with the Klan. Constructed in 1859 (and opening in 1869), the Maxwell House stood on the northeast corner of Fourth Avenue North and Church Street, in downtown Nashville, Tennessee. One of the city's most popular establishments, it was noted for its grand Christmas dinners and the visits of seven

U.S. presidents. One of them, Theodore Roosevelt, said that the Maxwell House's coffee was "good to the last drop," which became the famous slogan for America's first blended coffee. Other illustrious guests included Thomas Edison, William F. "Buffalo Bill" Cody, and Henry Ford. Website: http://tennesseeencyclopedia.net/. The Maxwell House Hotel was built by Col. John Overton, Jr., who named it after his wife Harriet Virginia Maxwell. John's daughter, Martha Overton, married Jacob McGavock Dickinson, Sr. in Nashville. Jacob served as assistant attorney general under President Stephen Grover Cleveland and secretary of war under President William Howard Taft. Martha's grandfather, Judge John Overton, Sr., was the owner of Travellers Rest (in Nashville), used as headquarters by Rebel General John Bell Hood between the Battles of Franklin and Nashville in December 1864. The Judge, along with Andrew Jackson and General James Winchester (the grandfather of my cousin Confederate Col. Edmund Winchester Rucker), founded the city of Memphis, TN. Seabrook, TMCP, p. 537.

179. Ashdown and Caudill, p. 60.
180. Henry, FWMF, pp. 20, 442.
181. Horn, IE, p. 37.
182. Henry, FWMF, p. 443. Also see Morton, passim. As mentioned, Forrest and the KKK are indeed discussed in Morton's Appendix. However, the section dealing with this topic was not contributed by Morton, but by others. Of particular interest is the 1906 remark of Mr. T. W. Gregory, whose knowledge of the Reconstruction KKK was encyclopedic. "It is *believed* that the 'Grand Wizard' was Nathan Bedford Forrest," Gregory noted in a speech before the Arkansas Bar Association that year. (Morton, p. 342.) Nothing definitive, just theory.
183. Wyeth, LGNBF, p. 619.
184. Mathes, pp. 370-373.
185. Gordon was one of the unlucky 702 Rebels captured at the Battle of Franklin II, November 30, 1864.
186. Wills, p. 336.
187. Mathes, p. 373.
188. Lytle, p. 385.
189. According to the Reconstruction KKK's *Prescript*: "Any member who shall reveal or betray the secrets of this Order, shall suffer the extreme penalty of the law" (Article 10, Clause 10). Burton, p. 37.
190. Ashdown and Caudill, p. 61.
191. Rose, pp. 18-19.
192. W. Jones, p. 75.
193. Rose, pp. 55-59.
194. Horn, IE, pp. 362-363.
195. *Reports of the Committees of the Senate of the United States (for the Second Session of the Forty-second Congress)*, pp. 22, 33, 34. My paraphrasal.
196. Henry, FWMF, p. 448.
197. Kelly, Michael. "History Tells the Real Story of Forrest," *The Daily News Journal*, December 9, 2006.
198. *Report of the Joint Select Committee to Inquire into the Condition of Affairs in the Late Insurrectionary States*, pp. 453-454. Emphasis added.
199. Morton, p. 343.
200. W. Jones, p. 48. Emphasis added.
201. W. Jones, pp. 52-54. Emphasis added.
202. For more on the overwhelming white racism of the early Northern states, see Seabrook, EYWTATCWIS, passim; Seabrook, EYWTATACWIW, passim; Seabrook, ALSV, passim; Seabrook, TGYC, passim.
203. W. Jones, p. 55.
204. W. Jones, p. 55.
205. Hurst, p. 11.

206. W. Jones, p. 75.
207. Seabrook, ARB, pp. 451, 578.
208. Rose, p. 71.
209. Fry, p. 163.
210. See Fry, p. 173.
211. W. Jones, p. 49. Emphasis added.
212. Rose, pp. 22-23. Emphasis added.
213. W. Jones, p. 69.
214. Rose, p. 7.
215. Fleming, DHR, Vol. 1, pp. 319-320. Emphasis added.
216. For more on the U.S.A. as the Confederate States of America, see Seabrook, C101, passim.
217. Fleming, DHR, Vol. 1, pp. 321-326. Emphasis added.
218. MacDonald, pp. 500-504.
219. *The Century*, pp. 311-316; MacDonald, pp. 508-511.
220. MacDonald, pp. 514-518. Emphasis added.
221. MacDonald, pp. 529-530.
222. For more on this topic, see Seabrook, C101, passim; Seabrook, TGYC, passim.
223. For more on this topic, see Seabrook, EYWTATCWIW, passim.
224. For more on this topic, see Seabrook, EYWTATCWIW, passim; Seabrook, C101, passim.
225. For the facts about the Battle of Fort Pillow, see Seabrook, NBFATBOFP, passim.
226. For the facts on Confederate Vice President Alexander H. Stephens' "Cornerstone Speech," see Seabrook, EYWTAASIW, pp. 260-269.
227. For more on this topic, see Seabrook, EYWTAASIW, passim.
228. For more on this topic, see Seabrook, EYWTAASIW, passim.
229. For more on this topic, see Seabrook, EYWTAASIW, passim.
230. *Reconstruction: Speech of Thaddeus Stevens, Delivered in the City of Lancaster, September 7, 1865*. Lancaster, PA: The Examiner, 1865. Emphasis added.
231. The appalling ignorance surrounding Southern institutions like the Reconstruction KKK is highlighted by the fact that the Liberal mainstream continually targets men like Forrest due to their association with it. This even after Forrest repeatedly said and showed that he was a friend of the black man. Seabrook, ARB, p. 459.
232. Emphasis added. According to the author of the article, Mrs. Grace Meredith Newbill, of Pulaski, TN: "On the morning of May 1, 1917, there was unveiled in the town of Pulaski, Tenn., a handsome bronze tablet commemorative of the birth and organization of the Ku-Klux Klan in this town. The tablet is placed on the outer wall of the law office once occupied by Judge Thomas M. Jones, a former Confederate Congressman, and bears the following inscription: 'Ku-Klux Klan Organized in this the law office of Judge Thomas M. Jones, December 24, 1865. Names of original organizers: Calvin E. Jones, Frank O. McCord, Richard R. Reed, John B. Kennedy, John C. Lester, James R. Crowe.' The unveiling was under the direction of the local Chapter of the United Daughters of the Confederacy and was witnessed by about one thousand people, including the student body of Martin College and of the Pulaski High School. Members of the John A. Woldridge Camp and Bivouac were guests of honor. The office was beautifully decorated with red and white bunting and Confederate and United States flags. The Sam Davis monument on the public square was also decorated in the Confederate colors and evergreen wreaths. The program was begun by *Dixie* and *America* sung by the high-school children. Mr. Laps D. McCord, Sr., made a fine address on the origin and purpose of the Ku-Klux Klan. After this the Martin College girls sang *My Old Kentucky Home* and were followed by the Pulaski Quintet in *Tenting on the Old Camp Ground*. . . . The program was concluded by the singing of *How Firm a Foundation!* by the audience." *Confederate Veteran*, July 1917, Vol. 25, No. 7, p. 335.

Bibliography

Adams, Charles. *When in the Course of Human Events: Arguing the Case for Southern Secession.* Lanham, MD: Rowman and Littlefield, 2000.
Adams, Francis D., and Barry Sanders. *Alienable Rights: The Exclusion of African Americans in a White Man's Land, 1619-2000.* 2003. New York, NY: Perennial, 2004 ed.
"A Late Member." *The Oaths, Signs, Ceremonies and Objects of the Ku Klux Klan: A Full Expose.* Cleveland, OH: self-published, 1868.
Alexander, William T. *History of the Colored Race in America.* 1887. Kansas City, MO: Palmetto Publishing Co., 1899 ed.
Alotta, Robert I. *Civil War Justice: Union Army Executions Under Lincoln.* Shippensburg, PA: White Mane, 1989.
Ashdown, Paul, and Edward Caudill. *The Myth of Nathan Bedford Forrest.* 2005. Lanham, MD: Rowman and Littlefield, 2006 ed.
Barrow, Charles Kelly, J. H. Segars, and R. B. Rosenburg (eds.). *Black Confederates.* 1995. Gretna, LA: Pelican Publishing Co., 2001 ed.
——. *Forgotten Confederates: An Anthology About Black Southerners.* Saint Petersburg, FL: Southern Heritage Press, 1997.
Basler, Roy Prentice (ed.). *Abraham Lincoln: His Speeches and Writings.* 1946. New York, NY: Da Capo Press, 2001 ed.
—— (ed.). *The Collected Works of Abraham Lincoln.* 9 vols. New Brunswick, NJ: Rutgers University Press, 1953.
Beard, James Melville. *K.K.K. Sketches, Humorous and Didactic: Treating the More Important Events of the Ku Klux Klan Movement in the South.* Philadelphia, PA: Claxton, Remsen and Haffelfinger, 1877.
Benson, Al, Jr., and Walter Donald Kennedy. *Lincoln's Marxists.* Gretna, LA: Pelican Publishing Co., 2011.
Biedermann, Hans. *Dictionary of Symbolism: Cultural Icons and the Meanings Behind Them.* 1989. New York, NY: Facts on File, 1992 ed.
Blee, Kathleen M. *Women of the Klan: Racism and Gender in the 1920s.* 1991. Berkeley, CA: University of California Press, 1992 ed.
Bradley, Michael R. *Nathan Bedford Forrest's Escort and Staff.* Gretna, LA: Pelican Publishing Co., 2006.
Browder, Earl. *Lincoln and the Communists.* New York, NY: Workers Library Publishers, Inc., 1936.
Brown, William Wells. *The Negro in the American Rebellion: His Heroism and His Fidelity.* Boston, MA: Lee and Shephard, 1867.
Browning, Robert, M., Jr. *Forrest: The Confederacy's Relentless Warrior.* Dulles, VA: Brassey's, Inc., 2004.
Burton, Annie Cooper. *The Ku Klux Klan.* Los Angeles, CA: Warren T. Potter, 1916.
Cartmell, Donald. *Civil War 101.* New York, NY: Gramercy, 2001.
Chesterson, G. K. *What I Saw in America.* New York, NY: Dodd, Mead and Co., 1923.
Coburn, Frederick William. *Moses Greeley Parker, M.D.* Lowell, MA: self-published, 1921.
Colby, Frank Moore (ed.). *The New National Encyclopedia.* New York, NY: Dodd, Mead and Co., 1917 (second ed.).
Cornish, Dudley Taylor. *The Sable Arm: Black Troops in the Union Army, 1861-1865.* 1956. Lawrence, KS: University Press of Kansas, 1987 ed.
Current, Richard N. *The Lincoln Nobody Knows.* 1958. New York, NY: Hill and Wang, 1963 ed.

——. (ed.). *The Confederacy (Information Now Encyclopedia)*. 1993. New York, NY: Macmillan, 1998 ed.
Damer, Eyre. *When the Ku Klux Rode*. New York, NY: Neale Publishing, 1912.
Davis, Jefferson. *The Rise and Fall of the Confederate Government*. 2 vols. New York, NY: D. Appleton and Co., 1881.
Denney, Robert E. *The Civil War Years: A Day-by-Day Chronicle of the Life of a Nation*. 1992. New York, NY: Sterling Publishing Co., 1994 ed.
DiLorenzo, Thomas J. *The Real Lincoln: A New Look at Abraham Lincoln, His Agenda, and an Unnecessary War*. Three Rivers, MI: Three Rivers Press, 2003.
Dixon, Thomas, Jr. *The Failure of Protestantism in New York and Its Causes*. New York, NY: Victor O. A. Strauss, 1896.
——. *The Clansman: An Historical Romance of the Ku Klux Klan*. 1905. New York, NY: A. Wessels Co., 1907 ed.
Meriwether, Elizabeth Avery (written under the pseudonym "George Edmonds"). *Facts and Falsehoods Concerning the War on the South, 1861-1865*. Memphis, TN: A. R. Taylor and Co., 1904.
Encyclopedia Britannica: A New Survey of Human Knowledge. 1929. Chicago, IL: Encyclopedia Britannica, Inc., 1955 ed.
Faust, Patricia L. (ed.). *Historical Times Illustrated Encyclopedia of the Civil War*. New York, NY: Harper and Row, 1986.
Findlay, Bruce, and Esther Findlay. *Your Rugged Constitution: How America's House of Freedom is Planned and Built*. 1950. Stanford, CA: Stanford University Press, 1951 ed.
Fleming, Walter Lynwood. *Freedmen's Bureau Documents*. Morgantown, WV: self-published, 1904.
——. *Civil War and Reconstruction in Alabama*. New York, NY: The Columbia University Press, 1905.
——. *Documentary History of Reconstruction: Political, Military, Social, Religious, Educational and Industrial, 1865 to the Present Time*. 2 vols. Cleveland, OH: Arthur H. Clark Co., 1906.
Foote, Shelby. *The Civil War: A Narrative, Fort Sumter to Perryville, Vol. I*. 1958. New York, NY: Vintage, 1986, ed.
——. *The Civil War: A Narrative, Fredericksburg to Meridian, Vol. II*. 1963. New York, NY: Vintage, 1986, ed.
——. *The Civil War: A Narrative, Red River to Appomattox, Vol. III*. 1974. New York, NY: Vintage, 1986, ed.
Franklin, John Hope. *Reconstruction After the Civil War*. Chicago, IL: University of Chicago Press, 1961.
Fry, Henry Peck. *The Modern Ku Klux Klan*. Boston, MA: Small, Maynard, and Co., 1922.
Gragg, Rod. *The Illustrated Confederate Reader: Extraordinary Eyewitness Accounts by the Civil War's Southern Soldiers and Civilians*. New York, NY: Gramercy Books, 1989.
Grant, Ulysses Simpson. *Personal Memoirs of U. S. Grant*. 2 vols. 1885-1886. New York, NY: Charles L. Webster and Co., 1886.
Hancock, Richard R. *Hancock's Diary: Or, A History of the Second Tennessee Confederate Cavalry*. 2 vols in 1. Nashville, TN: Brandon Printing Co., 1887.
Henry, Robert Selph. *The Story of the Confederacy*. 1931. New York, NY: Konecky and Konecky, 1999 ed.
——. (ed.). *As They Saw Forrest: Some Recollections and Comments of Contemporaries*. 1956. Wilmington, NC: Broadfoot Publishing Co., 1991 ed.
——. *First with the Most: Forrest*. New York, NY: Konecky and Konecky, 1992.

Highsmith, Carol M. and Ted Landphair. *Civil War Battlefields and Landmarks: A Photographic Tour.* New York, NY: Random House, 2003.

Hitler, Adolf. *Mein Kampf.* 2 vols. 1925, 1926. New York: NY: Reynal and Hitchcock, 1941 English translation ed.

Horn, Stanley F. *Invisible Empire: The Story of the Ku Klux Klan, 1866-1871.* 1939. Montclair, NJ: Patterson Smith, 1969 ed.

Horwitz, Tony. *Confederates in the Attic: Dispatches from the Unfinished Civil War.* 1998. New York, NY: Vintage, 1999 ed.

Hurst, Jack. *Nathan Bedford Forrest: A Biography.* 1993. New York, NY: Vintage, 1994 ed.

Johnson, Ludwell H. *North Against South: The American Iliad, 1848-1877.* 1978. Columbia, SC: Foundation for American Education, 1993 ed.

Johnson, Robert Underwood, and Clarence Clough Buell (eds.). *Battles and Leaders of the Civil War.* 4 vols. 1884. New York, NY: The Century Co., 1888 ed.

Johnstone, Huger William. *Truth of War Conspiracy, 1861.* Idylwild, GA: H. W. Johnstone, 1921.

Jones, John William. *The Davis Memorial Volume; Or Our Dead President, Jefferson Davis and the World's Tribute to His Memory.* Richmond, VA: B. F. Johnson, 1889.

Jones, Winfield. *Story of the Ku Klux Klan.* Washington, D.C.: American Newspaper Syndicate, 1921.

Jones, Wilmer L. *Generals in Blue and Gray.* 2 vols. Westport, CT: Praeger, 2004.

Jordan, Thomas, and John P. Pryor. *The Campaigns of General Nathan Bedford Forrest and of Forrest's Cavalry.* New Orleans, LA: Blelock and Co., 1868.

Lalor, John Joseph (ed.). *Cyclopædia of Political Science, Political Economy, and of the Political History of the United States, by the Best American and European Writers.* Chicago, IL: Melbert B. Cary and Co., 1883.

Lee, Robert E., Jr. *Recollections and Letters of General Robert E. Lee.* New York, NY: Doubleday, Page and Co., 1904.

Leech, Margaret. *Reveille in Washington, 1860-1865.* 1941. Alexandria, VA: Time-Life Books, 1980 ed.

Lester, John C., and D. L. Wilson. *Ku Klux Klan: Its Origin, Growth, and Disbandment.* 1884. New York, NY: Neale Publishing, 1905 ed.

Long, E. B., and Barbara Long. *The Civil War Day By Day: An Almanac 1861-1865.* Cambridge, MA: Da Capo Press, 1971.

Lytle, Andrew Nelson. *Bedford Forrest and His Critter Company.* New York, NY: G. P. Putnam's Sons, 1931.

MacDonald, William (ed.). *Documentary Source Book of American History, 1606-1913.* 1908. New York, NY: Macmillan Co., 1918 ed.

Marchmont, John. *Thirty-Four Years: An American Story of Southern Life.* Philadelphia, PA: Claxton, Remsen and Haffelfinger, 1878.

Martinez, James Michael. *Carpetbaggers, Cavalry, and the Ku Klux Klan: Exposing the Invisible Empire During Reconstruction.* Lanham, MD: Rowman and Littlefield, 2007.

Mathes, Capt. J. Harvey. *General Forrest.* New York, NY: D. Appleton and Co., 1902.

McCarty, Burke (ed.). *Little Sermons In Socialism by Abraham Lincoln.* Chicago, IL: The Chicago Daily Socialist, 1910.

McFeely, William S. *Yankee Stepfather: General O. O. Howard and the Freedmen - The Story of a Civil War Promise to Former Slaves Made—and Broken.* 1968. New York, NY: W. W. Norton, 1994.

McPherson, Edward. *The Political History of the United States of America, During the Great Rebellion (From November 6, 1860, to July 4, 1864).* Washington, D.C.: Philp and Solomons,

1864.

———. *The Political History of the United States of America, During the Period of Reconstruction, (From April 15, 1865, to July 15, 1870,) Including a Classified Summary of the Legislation of the Thirty-ninth, Fortieth, and Forty-first Congresses*. Washington, D.C.: Solomons and Chapman, 1875.

McPherson, James M. *The Struggle for Equality: Abolitionists and the Negro in the Civil War and Reconstruction*. 1964. Princeton, NJ: Princeton University Press, 1992 ed.

———. *The Negro's Civil War: How American Negroes Felt and Acted During the War for the Union*. 1965. Chicago, IL: University of Illinois Press, 1982 ed.

———. *Battle Cry of Freedom: The Civil War Era*. Oxford, UK: Oxford University Press, 2003.

———. *The Atlas of the Civil War*. Philadelphia, PA: Courage Books, 2005.

McPherson, James M., and the staff of the *New York Times*. *The Most Fearful Ordeal: Original Coverage of the Civil War by Writers and Reporters of the New York Times*. New York, NY: St. Martin's Press, 2004.

Morton, John Watson. *The Artillery of Nathan Bedford Forrest's Cavalry*. Nashville, TN: The M. E. Church, 1909.

Mullen, Robert W. *Blacks in America's Wars: The Shift in Attitudes from the Revolutionary War to Vietnam*. 1973. New York, NY: Pathfinder, 1991 ed.

Nicolay, John George, and John Hay (eds.). *Abraham Lincoln: Complete Works*. 12 vols. New York, NY: The Century Co., 1907.

ORA (full title: *The War of the Rebellion: A Compilation of the Official Records of the Union and Confederate Armies*. (Multiple volumes.) Washington, D.C.: Government Printing Office, 1880.

ORN (full title: *Official Records of the Union and Confederate Navies in the War of the Rebellion*). (Multiple volumes.) Washington, D.C.: Government Printing Office, 1894.

Pollard, Edward A. *Southern History of the War*. 2 vols in 1. New York, NY: Charles B. Richardson, 1866.

———. *The Lost Cause*. 1867. Chicago, IL: E. B. Treat, 1890 ed.

———. *Lee and His Lieutenants: Comprising the Early Life, Public Services, and Campaigns of General Robert E. Lee and His Companions in Arms*. New York, NY: E. B. Treat, 1867.

———. *The Lost Cause Regained*. New York, NY: G. W. Carlton and Co., 1868.

———. *Life of Jefferson Davis, With a Secret History of the Southern Confederacy, Gathered "Behind the Scenes in Richmond."* Philadelphia, PA: National Publishing Co., 1869.

Quarles, Benjamin. *The Negro in the Civil War*. 1953. Cambridge, MA: Da Capo Press, 1988 ed.

Reports of Committees of the Senate of the United States (for the Thirty-eighth Congress). Washington, D.C.: Government Printing Office, 1864.

Report of the Joint Committee on Reconstruction (at the First Session, Thirty-ninth Congress). Washington, D.C.: Government Printing Office, 1866.

Report of the Joint Select Committee to Inquire into the Condition of Affairs in the Late Insurrectionary States. Washington, D.C.: Government Printing Office, 1872.

Reports of Committees of the Senate of the United States (for the Second Session of the Forty-second Congress). Washington, D.C.: Government Printing Office, 1872.

Richardson, James D. (ed.). *A Compilation of the Messages and Papers of the Confederacy*. 2 vols. Nashville, TN: United States Publishing Co., 1905.

Richardson, John Anderson. *Richardson's Defense of the South*. Atlanta, GA: A. B. Caldwell, 1914.

Richardson, William Thomas. *Historic Pulaski: Birthplace of the Ku Klux Klan, Scene of the Execution of Sam Davis*. Self-published, 1913.

Ridley, Bromfield Lewis. *Battles and Sketches of the Army of Tennessee*. Mexico, MO: Missouri

Printing and Publishing Co., 1906.
Robuck, J. E. *My Own Personal Experience and Observation as a Soldier in the Confederate Army During the Civil War, 1861-1865*. N.p: Leslie Print and Publishing Co., 1911.
Rogers, Joel Augustus. *The Ku Klux Spirit*. 1923. Baltimore, MD: Black Classic Press, 1980 ed.
Rose, S. E. F. *The Ku Klux Klan or Invisible Empire*. New Orleans, LA: L. Graham Co., 1914.
Rutherford, Mildred Lewis. *A Hand-book of Southern Authors From the Settlement of Jamestown, 1607, to Living Writers*. Atlanta, GA: Franklin-Turner Co., 1907.
Sachsman, David B., S. Kittrell Rushing, and Roy Morris, Jr. (eds.). *Words at War: The Civil War and American Journalism*. West Lafayette, IN: Purdue University Press, 2008.
Seabrook, Lochlainn. *Nathan Bedford Forrest: Southern Hero, American Patriot*. 2007. Franklin, TN: Sea Raven Press, 2015 ed.
———. *Abraham Lincoln: The Southern View*. 2007. Franklin, TN: Sea Raven Press, 2013 ed.
———. *The McGavocks of Carnton Plantation: A Southern History - Celebrating One of Dixie's Most Noble Confederate Families and Their Tennessee Home*. 2008. Franklin, TN: Sea Raven Press, 2011 ed.
———. *A Rebel Born: A Defense of Nathan Bedford Forrest*. 2010. Franklin, TN: Sea Raven Press, 2011 ed.
———. *A Rebel Born: The Screenplay*. Unpublished screenplay. Franklin, TN: Sea Raven Press.
———. *Everything You Were Taught About the Civil War is Wrong, Ask a Southerner!* 2010. Franklin, TN: Sea Raven Press, revised 2014 ed.
———. *The Quotable Jefferson Davis: Selections From the Writings and Speeches of the Confederacy's First President*. Franklin, TN: Sea Raven Press, 2011.
———. *Lincolnology: The Real Abraham Lincoln Revealed In His Own Words*. Franklin, TN: Sea Raven Press, 2011.
———. *The Unquotable Abraham Lincoln: The President's Quotes They Don't Want You To Know!* Franklin, TN: Sea Raven Press, 2011.
———. *The Quotable Nathan Bedford Forrest: Selections From the Writings and Speeches of the Confederacy's Most Brilliant Cavalryman*. Franklin, TN: Sea Raven Press, 2012.
———. *Give 'Em Hell Boys! The Complete Military Correspondence of Nathan Bedford Forrest*. Franklin, TN: Sea Raven Press, 2012.
———. *The Great Impersonator: 99 Reasons to Dislike Abraham Lincoln*. Franklin, TN: Sea Raven Press, 2012.
———. *Forrest! 99 Reasons to Love Nathan Bedford Forrest*. Franklin, TN: Sea Raven Press, 2012.
———. *The Alexander H. Stephens Reader: Excerpts From the Works of a Confederate Founding Father*. Franklin, TN: Sea Raven Press, 2013.
———. *Saddle, Sword, and Gun: A Biography of Nathan Bedford Forrest For Teens*. Franklin, TN: Sea Raven Press, 2013.
———. *Everything You Were Taught About American Slavery War is Wrong, Ask a Southerner!* Franklin, TN: Sea Raven Press, 2015.
———. *Confederacy 101: Amazing Facts You Never Knew About America's Oldest Political Tradition*. Franklin, TN: Sea Raven Press, 2015.
———. *The Great Yankee Coverup: What the North Doesn't Want You to Know About Lincoln's War!* Franklin, TN: Sea Raven Press, 2015.
———. *Confederate Flag Facts: What Every American Should Know About Dixie's Southern Cross*. Franklin, TN: Sea Raven Press, 2015.
———. *Nathan Bedford Forrest and the Battle of Fort Pillow: Yankee Myth, Confederate Fact*. Franklin, TN: Sea Raven Press, 2015.
———. *Nathan Bedford Forrest and African-Americans: Yankee Myth, Confederate Fact*. Franklin, TN: Sea Raven Press, 2016.

Sheppard, Eric William. *Bedford Forrest, The Confederacy's Greatest Cavalryman.* 1930. Dayton, OH: Morningside House, 1981 ed.
Sherman, William Tecumseh. *Memoirs of General William T. Sherman.* 2 vols. 1875. New York, NY: D. Appleton and Co., 1891 ed.
Smith, Page. *Trial by Fire: A People's History of the Civil War and Reconstruction.* New York, NY: McGraw-Hill, 1982.
Stephens, Alexander Hamilton. *Speech of Mr. Stephens, of Georgia, on the War and Taxation.* Washington, D.C.: J and G. Gideon, 1848.
——. *A Constitutional View of the Late War Between the States; Its Causes, Character, Conduct and Results.* 2 vols. Philadelphia, PA: National Publishing, Co., 1870.
——. *Recollections of Alexander H. Stephens: His Diary Kept When a Prisoner at Fort Warren, Boston Harbour, 1865.* New York, NY: Doubleday, Page, and Co., 1910.
Stern, Philip Van Doren (ed.). *The Life and Writings of Abraham Lincoln.* 1940. New York, NY: Modern Library, 2000 ed.
Taylor, Richard. *Destruction and Reconstruction: Personal Experiences of the Late War in the United States.* New York, NY: D. Appleton, 1879.
Terkel, Studs. *Hard Times: An Oral History of the Great Depression.* New York, NY: Avon, 1970.
The Century of Independence: Embracing a Collection, From Official Sources, of the Most Important Documents and Statistics Connected With the Political History of America. Indianapolis, IN: J. R. Hussey and Co., 1876.
Thomas, Emory M. *The Confederate Nation: 1861-1865.* New York, NY: Harper and Row, 1979.
Warner, Ezra J. *Generals in Gray: Lives of the Confederate Commanders.* 1959. Baton Rouge, LA: Louisiana State University Press, 1989 ed.
——. *Generals in Blue: Lives of the Union Commanders.* 1964. Baton Rouge, LA: Louisiana State University Press, 2006 ed.
Watts, Peter. *A Dictionary of the Old West.* 1977. New York, NY: Promontory Press, 1987 ed.
Wills, Brian Steel. *The Confederacy's Greatest Cavalryman: Nathan Bedford Forrest.* Lawrence, KS: University Press of Kansas, 1992.
Wilson, Thomas L. *Sufferings Endured For a Free Government: A History of the Cruelties and Atrocities of the Rebellion.* 1864. Philadelphia, PA: King and Baird, 1865 ed.
Wilson, Woodrow. *A History of the American People.* 10 vols. 1901. New York, NY: Harper and Brothers, 1918 ed.
Woods, Thomas E., Jr. *The Politically Incorrect Guide to American History.* Washington D.C.: Regnery, 2004.
Woodward, William E. *Meet General Grant.* 1928. New York, NY: Liveright Publishing, 1946 ed.
Wyeth, John Allan. *Life of General Nathan Bedford Forrest.* New York, NY: Harper and Brothers, 1899.
——. *That Devil Forrest* (redacted modern version of Wyeth's *Life of General Nathan Bedford Forrest*). 1959. Baton Rouge, LA: Louisiana State University Press, 1989 ed.

182   Nathan Bedford Forrest & the Ku Klux Klan

This drawing shows an African-American politician serving on the Georgia legislature during Reconstruction. He was not voted into office and he had absolutely no qualifications that would justify his position. In fact, he could not read, write, or even sign his name. How then did he end up in one of the most coveted political offices in the state? He was intentionally placed there by Liberal Yankee Reconstruction agents for the sole purpose of angering Southern whites and disrupting white Southern society. This unconstitutional display of Northern pretentiousness and power was the equivalent of kicking a man while he is down. No one should be surprised that most Southern whites reacted with bitterness and wrath at these types of actions by the North. After all, this was the Liberal Yankee's intention. Today's anti-South proponents teach that the white South's reaction was due to racism, European-American hatred of African-Americans. While every section of the country has its racists (in particular the Northern states), this was not the reason the majority of Southern Caucasians responded with dismay during the carpetbag-scallywag regime. It was because they had been living under Yankee dominance and Northern socioeconomic rule for many decades, almost since the formation of our country in 1781, a time when the U.S.A. was called "the Confederate States of America." Frustration over this authoritarian control by Northern Liberals—who always seemed to put their section before the rest of the country—came to a head in November 1864 with the election of big government, anti-South Liberal Abraham Lincoln. For Dixie there was only one solution to the Yankee's obsessive urge to hurt, goad, harass, taunt, provoke, and control the South: *secession*. Lincoln refused to abide by the Constitution and thus "war came." Halfway through the conflict Lincoln cunningly altered the character of the War to one of abolition, and Radical Northern Liberals began demanding "immediate and uncompensated emancipation" in the South. The South resisted this demand for the same reason it resisted the placing of illiterate blacks in her local governments: after years of Yankee bullying, the South decided it was time to make up her own mind about her social issues, including abolition, black civil rights, and the incorporation of African-Americans into white Southern society as fully equal citizens. It was not a matter of whether or not these issues should be implemented. After all, the American abolition movement had begun in the South, with the first recorded emancipation in the colonies occurring in Virginia in 1655. It was a matter of sectional autonomy and personal pride with the Southern people that they be allowed to make decisions for themselves, as to when and how to carry out their own policies regarding everything from slavery and racial equality, to finances and politics. This the North would not allow, and so Reconstruction came. The South's true racial attitude emerged later, however, when she elected America's first black governor: Lawrence Douglas Wilder of Virginia, the grandson of Southern slaves.

Index

Adams, Shelby L., 188
Aldrich, Judge, 74
Ames, Adelbert, 73
Anderson, Loni, 188
Arthur, King, 187
Atkins, Chet, 188
Bancroft, George, 154
Barnett, T. J., 44, 108
Beard, James M., 98
Beauregard, Pierre G. T., 136, 188
Beecher, Henry W., 50, 54, 55
Bernstein, Leonard, 188
Blair, Francis, Jr., 156
Blair, Francis, Sr., 156
Blair, Frank P., 21
Blair, Montgomery, 156
Bolling, Edith, 188
Boone, Daniel, 188
Boone, Pat, 188
Breckinridge, John C., 188
Brooke, Edward W., 188
Brooks, Mr., 79
Brooks, Preston S., 188
Brownlow, William G., 30, 40, 50, 52, 54, 105
Buchanan, Patrick J., 188
Buford, Abraham, 188
Burton, Annie C., 92
Butler, Andrew P., 188
Butler, Benjamin F., 51, 52, 84, 136
Calvin, John, 61
Campbell, Joseph, 187
Canby, Edward R. C., 75
Carson, Martha, 188
Carter, Theodrick, 188
Cash, Johnny, 188
Caudill, Benjamin E., 187
Chamberlain, Daniel H., 106
Charlemagne, King, 157
Chase, Salmon P., 54, 59
Cheairs, Nathaniel F., 188
Chesnut, Mary, 188
Clark, William, 188

Colfax, Schuyler, 135
Collis, Captain, 20
Combs, Bertram T., 188
Crawford, Cindy, 188
Crockett, Davy, 188
Cromwell, Oliver, 61
Crowe, James R., 57, 101, 109, 110
Cruise, Tom, 188
Cyrus, Billy R., 188
Cyrus, Miley, 188
Davis, Jefferson, 9, 10, 61, 62, 146, 187, 188
Davis, Sam, 168
Dewees, Mr., 82
Diffinbach, B. E., 18, 19
Dixon, Thomas, Jr., 15, 93, 95, 108, 119, 121, 127, 128, 131, 137, 141, 143, 159
Dixon, Thomas, Sr., 164
Doolittle, James R., 129
Duvall, Robert, 188
Edward I, King, 187
Edwards, Thomas "Tom", 19
Fontaine, Lamar, 53
Foote, Shelby, 187
Forbes, Christopher, 188
Forrest, Nathan B., 187, 188
Forrest, Nathan Bedford, 10, 12-20, 22, 25-27, 29, 30, 32, 34-37, 39-42, 45, 81, 93, 95, 101-105, 109, 111, 112, 114-116, 118, 125, 164, 165, 168, 186
Fry, Henry P., 96
Garfield, James A., 55, 70
Garrison, William L., 36
Gayheart, Rebecca, 188
George III, King, 9
Gilbert, C. C., 77
Gist, States R., 188
Gordon, George W., 15, 35, 102, 103, 110, 111, 188
Grant, Ulysses S., 49, 57, 67, 73, 74,

76, 79, 80, 91, 115, 135, 136, 186
Graves, Robert, 187
Grental, Colonel, 76
Griffith, Andy, 188
Griffith, David W., 93, 95
Grotius, Hugo, 152
Guaraldi, Vince, 188
Halleck, Henry W., 49, 149, 152
Hambright, Frederick, 164
Hampton, Wade, 140
Harding, William G., 188
Hatch, Edward, 18
Hatch, Orrin, 18
Hayes, Rutherford B., 97, 140
Hitler, Adolf, 186
Holden, William W., 162, 163
Hood, John B., 188
Hooker, C., 73
Howard, Oliver O., 20
Humphreys, Benjamin G., 73
Imes, John, 74
Jackson, Andrew, 188
Jackson, Henry R., 188
Jackson, Stonewall, 188
James, Frank, 188
James, Jesse, 188
Jefferson, Thomas, 188
Jenkins, Charles J., 73
Jent, Elias, Sr., 188
Jesus, 58, 130, 136, 168, 187
Joan of Arc, 136
John, Elton, 188
Johnson, Andrew, 20, 59, 65, 67, 122, 149, 156, 161
Johnston, Joseph E., 10
Jones, Calvin E., 110
Jones, J. Calvin, 101, 109
Jones, Thomas M., 110
Jones, Winfield, 65, 107, 115
Judd, Ashley, 188
Judd, Naomi, 188
Judd, Wynonna, 188
Kennedy, John B., 74, 101, 109, 110, 115
Kennedy, John B., Mrs., 110

Landrum, W. W., 112
Lee, Fitzhugh, 188
Lee, Robert E., 16, 27, 47, 51, 57, 136, 188
Lee, Stephen D., 188
Lee, William H. F., 188
Lester, John C., 101, 109, 110
Lewis, Meriwether, 188
Lincoln, Abraham, 9, 11-14, 17, 18, 22, 26-29, 44, 46, 54, 56, 59, 61, 62, 98, 104, 108, 115, 123, 136, 145, 154, 156, 160, 186
Lincoln, Andrew, 156
Longstreet, James, 10, 27, 188
Loveless, Patty, 188
Luther, Martin, 61
Lycurgus of Sparta, 157
Manigault, Arthur M., 188
Manigault, Joseph, 188
Martin, Laura, 43
Martin, Thomas, 111
Marvin, Lee, 188
Marx, Karl, 186
Mathes, J. Harvey, 102
Maury, Abram P., 188
McAfee, Leroy, 128, 163
McArdle, Mr., 77
McCord, Frank O., 101, 109, 110
McGavock, Caroline E., 188
McGavock, David H., 188
McGavock, Emily, 188
McGavock, Francis, 188
McGavock, James R., 188
McGavock, John W., 188
McGavock, Lysander, 188
McGavock, Randal W., 188
McGraw, Tim, 188
Meade, George, 74
Meriwether, Elizabeth A., 71, 188
Meriwether, Minor, 15, 188
Milton, John, 136
Montgomery, Mary Ann, 18
Morgan, John H., 188
Morton, John W., 15, 102, 125, 165, 188

Morton, Oliver P., 85, 88
Mosby, John S., 50, 188
Myers, Jasper, 73
Napoleon I, 160
Newbill, Grace M., 110
Nugent, Ted, 188
Ord, Edward O. C., 77
Page, Thomas N., 91, 92
Paine, Ora Susan, 15, 102
Parsons, Theophilus, 153
Parton, Dolly, 188
Pettus, Edmund W., 188
Phillimore, Robert, 152
Phillips, Wendell, 50, 72, 73
Piatt, Abram S., 73
Pike, Albert, 130
Pillow, Gideon J., 188
Polk, James K., 188
Polk, Leonidas, 188
Polk, Lucius E., 188
Presley, Elvis, 188
Pufendorf, Samuel von, 152
Randolph, Edmund J., 188
Randolph, George W., 188
Reagan, Ronald, 188
Reed, Richard R., 101, 109, 110
Reynolds, Burt, 188
Robbins, Hargus, 188
Robert the Bruce, King, 187
Roosevelt, Theodore, 97
Rose, S. E. F., 43, 61, 64, 112
Rucker, Edmund W., 22, 188
Russell, Lord, 147
Scott, George C., 188
Scruggs, Earl, 188
Seabrook, John L., 188
Seabrook, Lochlainn, 13, 14, 16, 187, 188, 190
Seger, Bob, 188
Semmes, Raphael, 146
Senter, DeWitt C., 40
Shellabarger, Samuel, 129
Sheridan, Philip H., 49, 80
Sherman, William T., 18, 123, 124, 140
Simmons, William J., 41, 48, 49, 113, 166
Skaggs, Ricky, 188
Stephens, Alexander H., 9, 10, 188
Stevens, Thaddeus, 57, 84-86, 97, 98, 108, 160, 161, 164
Stewart, Alexander P., 188
Stokes, Mr., 81
Stoneman, Austin, 108
Stuart, Jeb, 188
Sumner, Charles, 66
Sumners, George, 70
Taylor, Richard, 10, 188
Taylor, Sarah K., 188
Taylor, Zachary, 188
Tocqueville, Alexis de, 32
Tourgee, Albion W., 162, 163
Turner, Nat, 36
Tynes, Ellen B., 125, 188
Vance, Robert B., 188
Vance, Zebulon, 188
Vattel, Emer de, 149, 152
Venable, Charles S., 188
Wade, Benjamin F., 85, 86, 135
Washburn, Mr., 82
Washington, George, 9, 157
Washington, John A., 188
Washington, Thornton A., 188
Webster, Daniel, 136
Webster, Mr., 78
Weitzel, Godfrey, 52
Wilder, Lawrence D., 182
Wilson, Woodrow, 82, 86, 88, 91, 92, 188
Winder, Charles S., 188
Winder, John H., 188
Wirz, Henry, 149
Witherspoon, Reese, 188
Womack, John B., 188
Womack, Lee Ann, 188
Woodward, Mr., 82
Wyeth, John Allan, 15, 102
Yates, Richard, 51, 52
Zollicoffer, Felix K., 188

One of the few pro-South cartoons that has survived from the Reconstruction period, this 1875 wood engraving is entitled: "Grant's Last Outrage in Louisiana." It shows President Ulysses S. Grant using Federal troops to illegally oust the entire legislature of Louisiana, so he can replace them with carpetbaggers and uneducated blacks. Uncle Sam (symbolizing the U.S. Constitution) says to Grant: "Hold there! Hold there, General! I have tolerated the abuses of your office long enough." Grant replies: "March those legislators out. I am going to have my way in this matter." The headline of the newspaper lying on the ground reads: "We are in the midst of a revolution tending fast to the concentration of all power in the hands of one man." Dictatorships, of course, have always been a favorite of Liberals and socialists, which is exactly what Reconstruction turned out to be: a monarchical tyranny with Grant at the helm and the U.S. Constitution trampled and in tatters. Lincoln was of the same mind, which is why he surrounded himself with Marxists, was idolized by Karl Marx himself, was widely supported and quoted by socialists, appointed socialists and communists to his administration and the Union army, and was adored by fellow dictators like Adolf Hitler, leader of the NAZIS—an acronym for the "National Socialist German Workers Party." Forrest and the members of the Reconstruction KKK, on the other hand, were conservatives, patriots, and strict constitutionalists who championed traditional American values: love of God, family, and country.

MEET THE AUTHOR

"ASKING THE PATRIOTIC SOUTH TO STOP HONORING HER CONFEDERATE ANCESTORS IS LIKE ASKING THE SUN NOT TO SHINE." — COLONEL LOCHLAINN SEABROOK

LOCHLAINN SEABROOK, a Kentucky Colonel and the winner of the prestigious Jefferson Davis Historical Gold Medal for his "masterpiece," *A Rebel Born: A Defense of Nathan Bedford Forrest*, is an unreconstructed Southern historian, award-winning author, Civil War scholar, Bible authority, and traditional Southern Agrarian of Scottish, English, Irish, Dutch, Welsh, German, and Italian extraction.

A child prodigy, Seabrook is today a true Renaissance Man whose occupational titles also include encyclopedist, lexicographer, musician, artist, graphic designer, genealogist, photographer, and award-winning poet. Also a songwriter and a screenwriter, he has a 40 year background in historical nonfiction writing and is a member of the Sons of Confederate Veterans, the Civil War Trust, and the National Grange.

Due to similarities in their writing styles, ideas, and literary works, Seabrook is often referred to as the "new Shelby Foote," the "Southern Joseph Campbell," and the "American Robert Graves" (his English cousin). Seabrook coined the term "South-shaming," and holds the world's record for writing the most books on Nathan Bedford Forrest: nine. In addition, Seabrook is the first Civil War scholar to connect the early American nickname for the U.S., "The Confederate States of America," with the Southern Confederacy that arose eight decades later, and the first to note that in 1860 the party platforms of the two major political parties were the opposite of what they are today (Victorian Democrats were conservatives, Victorian Republicans were liberals).

The grandson of an Appalachian coal-mining family, Seabrook is a seventh-generation Kentuckian, co-chair of the Jent/Gent Family Committee (Kentucky), founder and director of the Blakeney Family Tree Project, and a board member of the Friends of Colonel Benjamin E. Caudill. Seabrook's literary works have been endorsed by leading authorities, museum curators, award-winning historians, bestselling authors, celebrities, noted scientists, well respected educators, TV show hosts and producers, renowned military artists, esteemed Southern organizations, and distinguished academicians from around the world.

Seabrook has authored over 50 popular adult books on the American Civil War, American and international slavery, the U.S. Confederacy (1781), the Southern Confederacy (1861), religion, theology and thealogy, Jesus, the Bible, the Apocrypha, the Law of Attraction, alternative health, spirituality, ghost stories, the paranormal, ufology, social issues, and cross-cultural studies of the family and marriage. His Confederate biographies, pro-South studies, genealogical monographs, family histories, military encyclopedias, self-help guides, and etymological dictionaries have received wide acclaim.

Seabrook's eight children's books include a Southern guide to the Civil War, a biography of Nathan Bedford Forrest, a dictionary of religion and myth, a rewriting of the King Arthur legend (which reinstates the original pre-Christian motifs), two bedtime stories for preschoolers, a naturalist's guidebook to owls, a worldwide look at the family, and an examination of the Near-Death Experience.

Of blue-blooded Southern stock through his Kentucky, Tennessee, Virginia, West Virginia, and North Carolina ancestors, he is a direct descendant of European royalty via his 6th great-grandfather, the Earl of Oxford, after which London's famous Harley Street is named. Among his celebrated male Celtic ancestors is Robert the Bruce, King of Scotland, Seabrook's 22nd great-grandfather. The 21st great-grandson of Edward I "Longshanks" Plantagenet), King of England, Seabrook is a thirteenth-generation Southerner through his descent from the colonists of Jamestown, Virginia (1607).

The 2nd, 3rd, and 4th great-grandson of dozens of Confederate soldiers, one of his closest connections to Lincoln's War is through his 3rd great-grandfather, Elias Jent, Sr., who fought for the Confederacy in the

Above, Colonel Lochlainn Seabrook, award-winning Civil War scholar and unreconstructed Southern historian. America's most popular and prolific pro-South author, his many books have introduced hundreds of thousands to the truth about the War for Southern Independence. He coined the phrase "South-shaming" and holds the world's record for writing the most books on Nathan Bedford Forrest.

Thirteenth Cavalry Kentucky under Seabrook's 2nd cousin, Colonel Benjamin E. Caudill. The Thirteenth, also known as "Caudill's Army," fought in numerous conflicts, including the Battles of Saltville, Gladsville, Mill Cliff, Poor Fork, Whitesburg, and Leatherwood.

Seabrook is a direct descendant of the families of Alexander H. Stephens, John Singleton Mosby, William Giles Harding, and Edmund Winchester Rucker, and is related to the following Confederates and other 18th- and 19th-Century luminaries: Robert E. Lee, Stephen Dill Lee, Stonewall Jackson, Nathan Bedford Forrest, James Longstreet, John Hunt Morgan, Jeb Stuart, Pierre G. T. Beauregard (approved the Confederate Battle Flag design), George W. Gordon, John Bell Hood, Alexander Peter Stewart, Arthur M. Manigault, Joseph Manigault, Charles Scott Venable, Thornton A. Washington, John A. Washington, Abraham Buford, Edmund W. Pettus, Theodrick "Tod" Carter, John B. Womack, John H. Winder, Gideon J. Pillow, States Rights Gist, Henry R. Jackson, John Lawton Seabrook, John C. Breckinridge, Leonidas Polk, Zachary Taylor, Sarah Knox Taylor (first wife of Jefferson Davis), Richard Taylor, Davy Crockett, Daniel Boone, Meriwether Lewis (of the Lewis and Clark Expedition) Andrew Jackson, James K. Polk, Abram Poindexter Maury (founder of Franklin, TN), Zebulon Vance, Thomas Jefferson, Edmund Jennings Randolph, George Wythe Randolph (grandson of Jefferson), Felix K. Zollicoffer, Fitzhugh Lee, Nathaniel F. Cheairs, Jesse James, Frank James, Robert Brank Vance, Charles Sidney Winder, John W. McGavock, Caroline E. (Winder) McGavock, David Harding McGavock, Lysander McGavock, James Randal McGavock, Randal William McGavock, Francis McGavock, Emily McGavock, William Henry F. Lee, Lucius E. Polk, Minor Meriwether (husband of noted pro-South author Elizabeth Avery Meriwether), Ellen Bourne Tynes (wife of Forrest's chief of artillery, Captain John W. Morton), South Carolina Senators Preston Smith Brooks and Andrew Pickens Butler, and famed South Carolina diarist Mary Chesnut.

(Photo © Lochlainn Seabrook)

Seabrook's modern day cousins include: Patrick J. Buchanan (conservative author), Cindy Crawford (model), Shelby Lee Adams (Letcher Co., Kentucky, photographer), Bertram Thomas Combs (Kentucky's 50th governor), Edith Bolling (wife of President Woodrow Wilson), and actors Andy Griffith, George C. Scott, Robert Duvall, Reese Witherspoon, Lee Marvin, Rebecca Gayheart, and Tom Cruise.

Seabrook's screenplay, *A Rebel Born*, based on his book of the same name, has been signed with acclaimed filmmaker Christopher Forbes (of Forbes Film). It is now in pre-production, and is set for release in 2017 as a full-length feature film. This will be the first movie ever made of Nathan Bedford Forrest's life story, and as a historically accurate project written from the Southern perspective, is destined to be one of the most talked about Civil War films of all time.

Born with music in his blood, Seabrook is an award-winning, multi-genre, BMI-Nashville songwriter and lyricist who has composed some 3,000 songs (250 albums), and whose original music has been heard in film (*A Rebel Born, Cowgirls 'n Angels, Confederate Cavalry, Billy the Kid: Showdown in Lincoln County, Vengeance Without Mercy, Last Step, County Line, The Mark*) and on TV and radio worldwide. A musician, producer, multi-instrumentalist, and renown performer—whose keyboard work has been variously compared to pianists from Hargus Robbins and Vince Guaraldi to Elton John and Leonard Bernstein—Seabrook has opened for groups such as the Earl Scruggs Review, Ted Nugent, and Bob Seger, and has performed privately for such public figures as President Ronald Reagan, Burt Reynolds, Loni Anderson, and Senator Edward W. Brooke. Seabrook's cousins in the music business include: Johnny Cash, Elvis Presley, Billy Ray and Miley Cyrus, Patty Loveless, Tim McGraw, Lee Ann Womack, Dolly Parton, Pat Boone, Naomi, Wynonna, and Ashley Judd, Ricky Skaggs, the Sunshine Sisters, Martha Carson, and Chet Atkins.

Seabrook lives with his wife and family in historic Middle Tennessee, the heart of Forrest country and the Confederacy, where his conservative Southern ancestors fought valiantly against Liberal Lincoln and the progressive North in defense of Jeffersonianism, constitutional government, and personal liberty.

LOCHLAINNSEABROOK.COM

LOCHLAINN SEABROOK   189

If you enjoyed this book you will be interested in Mr. Seabrook's other popular Civil War related titles:

☛ EVERYTHING YOU WERE TAUGHT ABOUT THE CIVIL WAR IS WRONG, ASK A SOUTHERNER!
☛ EVERYTHING YOU WERE TAUGHT ABOUT AMERICAN SLAVERY IS WRONG, ASK A SOUTHERNER!
☛ CONFEDERATE FLAG FACTS: WHAT EVERY AMERICAN SHOULD KNOW ABOUT DIXIE'S SOUTHERN CROSS
☛ CONFEDERACY 101: AMAZING FACTS YOU NEVER KNEW ABOUT AMERICA'S OLDEST POLITICAL TRADITION

Available from Sea Raven Press and wherever fine books are sold

ALL OF OUR BOOK COVERS ARE AVAILABLE AS 11" X 17" POSTERS, SUITABLE FOR FRAMING.

SeaRavenPress.com • NathanBedfordForrestBooks.com

www.ingramcontent.com/pod-product-compliance
Lightning Source LLC
Chambersburg PA
CBHW031259110426
42743CB00041B/743